Brave and Blessed

A Year of Devotions and Affirmations for Kids

T.L.S. Jones

© **Copyright 2024 - All rights reserved.**

The content contained within this book may not be reproduced, duplicated or transmitted without direct written permission from the author or the publisher.

Under no circumstances will any blame or legal responsibility be held against the publisher, or author, for any damages, reparation, or monetary loss due to the information contained within this book, either directly or indirectly.

Legal Notice:

This book is copyright protected. It is only for personal use. You cannot amend, distribute, sell, use, quote or paraphrase any part, or the content within this book, without the consent of the author or publisher.

Disclaimer Notice:

Please note the information contained within this document is for educational and entertainment purposes only. All effort has been executed to present accurate, up to date, reliable, complete information. No warranties of any kind are declared or implied. Readers acknowledge that the author is not engaged in the rendering of legal, financial, medical or professional advice. The content within this book has been derived from various sources. Please consult a licensed professional before attempting any techniques outlined in this book.

By reading this document, the reader agrees that under no circumstances is the author responsible for any losses, direct or indirect, that are incurred as a result of the use of the information contained within this document, including, but not limited to, errors, omissions, or inaccuracies.

Table of Contents

INTRODUCTION 1

BEFORE YOU START 3
    How to Practice Meditation? 3
    Prayer and Devotion 3
    Journaling 4

WEEK 1: GOD'S AMAZING WORLD 5
    Day 1: The Beginning of Everything 5
    Day 2: Light and Darkness 6
    Day 3: The Sky and the Waters 7
    Day 4: Land and Plants 8
    Day 5: The Sun, Moon, and Stars 9
    Day 6: Creatures of the Sea and Sky 10
    Day 7: End-Of-Week Review 11

WEEK 2: FAITH: TRUSTING GOD IN EVERYTHING 13
    Day 1: What Is Faith? 13
    Day 2: Faith in Action 14
    Day 3: Trusting God in Tough Times 15
    Day 4: God's" Promises 15
    Day 5: Helping Others Trust God 16
    Day 6: Faith Like a Child 17
    Day 7: End-Of-Week Review 18

WEEK 3: PRAYER: TALKING TO GOD ANYWHERE 19
    Day 1: What Is Prayer? 19
    Day 2: Types of Prayer 20
    Day 3: Prayer Warriors 21
    Day 4: Listening to God 21
    Day 5: Thankful Prayers 22
    Day 6: Praying Together 23
    Day 7: End-Of-Week Review 23

WEEK 4: FORGIVENESS: LETTING GO OF GRUDGES 25
    Day 1: Understanding Forgiveness 25
    Day 2: Jesus Forgives Us 26
    Day 3: The Importance of Forgiveness 27
    Day 4: Forgiving Ourselves 28
    Day 5: Acts of Kindness 28
    Day 6: Letting Go of Grudges 29
    Day 7: End-Of-Week Review 30

WEEK 5: KINDNESS: MAKING A DIFFERENCE EVERY DAY 31
    Day 1: What Is Kindness? 31

- DAY 2: THE KINDNESS OF JESUS 32
- DAY 3: RANDOM ACTS OF KINDNESS 33
- DAY 4: KINDNESS IN OUR WORDS 34
- DAY 5: SHARING KINDNESS IN OUR COMMUNITY 35
- DAY 6: THE RIPPLE EFFECT OF KINDNESS 36
- DAY 7: END-OF-WEEK REVIEW 36

WEEK 6: GRATITUDE: THANKING GOD FOR HIS BLESSINGS 39
- DAY 1: WHAT IS GRATITUDE? 39
- DAY 2: COUNTING OUR BLESSINGS 40
- DAY 3: THANKFULNESS IN HARD TIMES 41
- DAY 4: GRATITUDE IN PRAYER 42
- DAY 5: SHARING GRATITUDE 43
- DAY 6: THANKFULNESS FOR CREATION 44
- DAY 7: END-OF-WEEK REVIEW 45

WEEK 7: PATIENCE: WAITING FOR GOD'S PERFECT TIMING 47
- DAY 1: WHAT IS PATIENCE? 47
- DAY 2: GOD'S TIMING IS PERFECT 48
- DAY 3: WAITING ON GOD 49
- DAY 4: THE REWARDS OF PATIENCE 49
- DAY 5: PATIENCE IN RELATIONSHIPS 50
- DAY 6: GOD'S WAITING ROOM 51
- DAY 7: END-OF-WEEK REVIEW 52

WEEK 8: SERVING OTHERS: HELPING WITH A HAPPY HEART 53
- DAY 1: THE CALL TO SERVE 53
- DAY 2: KINDNESS IN ACTION 54
- DAY 3: SERVING WITH A HAPPY HEART 55
- DAY 4: HELPING AT HOME 55
- DAY 5: SERVING IN OUR COMMUNITY 56
- DAY 6: TEAMWORK IN SERVICE 57
- DAY 7: END-OF-WEEK REVIEW 58

WEEK 9: JOY: FINDING HAPPINESS IN GOD'S PRESENCE 59
- DAY 1: WHAT IS JOY? 59
- DAY 2: JOY IN DIFFICULT TIMES 60
- DAY 3: SHARING JOY 61
- DAY 4: JOYFUL PRAISE 62
- DAY 5: JOY IN CREATION 62
- DAY 6: JOY THROUGH GRATITUDE 64
- DAY 7: END-OF-WEEK REVIEW 65

WEEK 10: PEACE: CALM IN THE STORM 67
- DAY 1: WHAT IS PEACE? 67
- DAY 2: FINDING PEACE IN PRAYER 68
- DAY 3: PEACE IN DIFFICULT TIMES 69
- DAY 4: SHARING PEACE WITH OTHERS 70
- DAY 5: TRUSTING GOD FOR PEACE 70
- DAY 6: PEACE IN NATURE 72

DAY 7: END-OF-WEEK REVIEW 72

WEEK 11: HOPE: BELIEVING IN BETTER DAYS 75

DAY 1: WHAT IS HOPE? 75
DAY 2: HOPE IN GOD'S PROMISES 76
DAY 3: HOPE IN DIFFICULT TIMES 77
DAY 4: SHARING HOPE WITH OTHERS 78
DAY 5: HOPE THROUGH PRAYER 78
DAY 6: HOPE IN COMMUNITY 79
DAY 7: END-OF-WEEK REVIEW 80

WEEK 12: COURAGE: STANDING STRONG FOR GOD 81

DAY 1: WHAT IS COURAGE? 81
DAY 2: COURAGE IN FAITH 82
DAY 3: COURAGE TO STAND UP FOR OTHERS 83
DAY 4: THE COURAGE OF DANIEL 84
DAY 5: COURAGE TO SHARE YOUR FAITH 84
DAY 6: COURAGE IN EVERYDAY LIFE 85
DAY 7: END-OF-WEEK REVIEW 86

WEEK 13: HONESTY: SPEAKING THE TRUTH IN LOVE 87

DAY 1: WHAT IS HONESTY? 87
DAY 2: HONESTY WITH OURSELVES 88
DAY 3: HONESTY IN RELATIONSHIPS 89
DAY 4: THE IMPORTANCE OF TRUTH 90
DAY 5: SPEAKING THE TRUTH IN LOVE 90
DAY 6: FORGIVENESS AND HONESTY 92
DAY 7: END-OF-WEEK REVIEW 93

WEEK 14: LOVE: THE GREATEST COMMANDMENT 95

DAY 1: WHAT IS LOVE? 95
DAY 2: GOD'S" LOVE FOR US 96
DAY 3: LOVING OTHERS 97
DAY 4: LOVE IN ACTION 97
DAY 5: LOVE AND FORGIVENESS 98
DAY 6: LOVING YOUR ENEMIES 99
DAY 7: END-OF-WEEK REVIEW 100

WEEK 15: OBEDIENCE: FOLLOWING GOD'S WORD 101

DAY 1: WHAT IS OBEDIENCE? 101
DAY 2: GOD CAN SHOW YOU THE WAY—TRUST HIM 102
DAY 3: LOVING AND RESPECTING YOUR PARENTS 103
DAY 4: BE BRAVE LIKE JESUS 104
DAY 5: OBEYING GOD LEADS TO HAPPINESS AND PEACE 105
DAY 6: LEARNING FROM OUR MISTAKES 106
DAY 7: END-OF-WEEK REVIEW 107

WEEK 16: HUMILITY: BEING MODEST AND RESPECTFUL 109

DAY 1: WHAT IS HUMILITY? 109
DAY 2: SERVE OTHERS AS JESUS DID 110

- Day 3: Being a Good Friend 111
- Day 4: Being a Good Listener 112
- Day 5: We Should Thank God for Our Blessings 112
- Day 6: Helping Others Is an Act of Love 113
- Day 7: End-Of-Week Review 114

WEEK 17: GENEROSITY: GIVING FROM THE HEART 115

- Day 1: What Is Generosity? 115
- Day 2: True Abundance 116
- Day 3: Showing True Generosity 117
- Day 4: Sharing Is Caring 118
- Day 5: Giving Time to Help Others 119
- Day 6: Encouraging Others With Kind Words 120
- Day 7: End-Of-Week Review 120

WEEK 18: FAITHFULNESS: KEEPING YOUR PROMISES 123

- Day 1: Celebrate God's Faithfulness 123
- Day 2: Being Grateful for God's Faithfulness 124
- Day 3: Keeping Promises 125
- Day 4: Doing My Best in Everything I Do 126
- Day 5: Being Faithful in Our Prayers 126
- Day 6: Following God Faithfully 127
- Day 7: End-Of-Week Review 128

WEEK 19: SELF-CONTROL: MAKING RIGHT CHOICES 129

- Day 1: What Is Self-Control? 129
- Day 2: Making Good Decisions 130
- Day 3: Conquering Temptation With Jesus 131
- Day 4: Thinking Before Speaking 132
- Day 5: Remaining Calm and Patient 133
- Day 6: Pleasing God Through Self-Control 134
- Day 7: End-Of-Week Review 135

WEEK 20: CONTENTMENT: BEING HAPPY WITH WHAT YOU HAVE 137

- Day 1: What Is Contentment? 137
- Day 2: Cherish Your Blessings 138
- Day 3: Showing Love and Appreciation to Your Friends and Family 139
- Day 4: Appreciating God's Creation 140
- Day 5: Finding Joy in Sharing 141
- Day 6: Thank You, God 142
- Day 7: End-Of-Week Review 142

WEEK 21: FRIENDSHIP: LOVING AND SUPPORTING EACH OTHER 145

- Day 1: The Power of Friendship 145
- Day 2: Support Your Friends 146
- Day 3: Share Joy With Friends 147
- Day 4: Forgiving Each Other 148
- Day 5: Being a Good Listener 148
- Day 6: Encouraging Each Other 150
- Day 7: End-Of-Week Review 150

WEEK 22: WORSHIP: HONORING GOD IN EVERYTHING 153
- DAY 1: HOW TO WORSHIP GOD 153
- DAY 2: GOD LOVES WHEN WE WORSHIP HIM JOYFULLY! 154
- DAY 3: WORSHIPPING GOD THROUGH OUR GOOD ACTIONS 155
- DAY 4: WORSHIPPING GOD SINCERELY 156
- DAY 5: PRAISING GOD 156
- DAY 6: WORSHIPING GOD THROUGH GRATITUDE 157
- DAY 7: END-OF-WEEK REVIEW 158

WEEK 23: WISDOM: LISTENING TO GOD'S GUIDANCE 159
- DAY 1: WHAT IS WISDOM? 159
- DAY 2: GOD SPEAKS TO US THROUGH HIS WORD 160
- DAY 3: ASKING GOD FOR GUIDANCE 161
- DAY 4: LISTENING TO WISE PEOPLE 162
- DAY 5: TRUSTING GOD 163
- DAY 6: HUMILITY AND WISDOM 164
- DAY 7: END-OF-WEEK REVIEW 164

WEEK 24: GOD'S LOVE: UNCONDITIONAL AND EVERLASTING 167
- DAY 1: EMBRACED BY GOD'S LOVE 167
- DAY 2: GOD'S LOVE IS EVERLASTING 168
- DAY 3: LOVING OTHERS 169
- DAY 4: GOD COMFORTS ME 170
- DAY 5: LOVING EACH OTHER 171
- DAY 6: CELEBRATING GOD 172
- DAY 7: END-OF-WEEK REVIEW 173

WEEK 25: THE BIBLE: LEARNING FROM GOD'S WORDS 175
- DAY 1: READING THE BIBLE TO KNOW GOD 175
- DAY 2: THE BIBLE IS MY SOURCE OF WISDOM 176
- DAY 3: EMBRACING GOD'S WORDS 177
- DAY 4: GOD'S WORDS PROVIDE COMFORT AND HOPE 178
- DAY 5: DISCIPLESHIP 178
- DAY 6: ASKING QUESTIONS 179
- DAY 7: END-OF-WEEK REVIEW 180

WEEK 26: THE HOLY SPIRIT: OUR HELPER AND GUIDE 183
- DAY 1: THE HOLY SPIRIT HELPS YOU 183
- DAY 2: THE HOLY SPIRIT ALWAYS LISTENS TO US 184
- DAY 3: I AM BRAVE AND STRONG WITH THE HOLY SPIRIT BY MY SIDE 185
- DAY 4: THE HOLY SPIRIT TEACHES ME ABOUT GOD 186
- DAY 5: TRUSTING THE HOLY SPIRIT 187
- DAY 6: THE FRUITS OF THE SPIRIT 188
- DAY 7: SHARING GOD'S LOVE 189

WEEK 27: COMMUNITY: BEING PART OF GOD'S FAMILY 191
- DAY 1: CARING FOR EACH OTHER 191
- DAY 2: USING MY GIFTS 192
- DAY 3: ENCOURAGING ONE ANOTHER 193

- Day 4: Loving Everyone 194
- Day 5: Supporting Those in Need 194
- Day 6: Feeling Joyful for My Community 195
- Day 7: End-Of-Week Review 196

WEEK 28: CELEBRATING GOD'S GOODNESS 197
- Day 1: God Is Good 197
- Day 2: Being Thankful 198
- Day 3: God Loves Everyone 198
- Day 4: Singing to the Lord 199
- Day 5: Sharing God's Goodness 199
- Day 6: Acknowledging God's Goodness 200
- Day 7: End-Of-Week Review 201

WEEK 29: COMPASSION: CARING FOR THOSE IN NEED 203
- Day 1: What Is Compassion? 203
- Day 2: Being Compassionate 204
- Day 3: Understanding Others' Feelings 205
- Day 4: Sharing Kind Words 205
- Day 5: Practicing Compassion Each Day 206
- Day 6: Supporting Others With Compassion 207
- Day 7: End-Of-Week Review 208

WEEK 30: IDENTITY IN CHRIST: UNDERSTANDING WHO WE ARE 209
- Day 1: Our True Identity 209
- Day 2: Being Renewed 210
- Day 3: Redemption 211
- Day 4: God Has Plans for Me 212
- Day 5: We Are Part of God's Family 212
- Day 6: Being God's Light 213
- Day 7: End-Of-Week Review 214

WEEK 31: THE IMPORTANCE OF CHURCH: GATHERING TO GROW 215
- Day 1: Going to Church 215
- Day 2: Being Part of My Community 216
- Day 3: Hearing the Words of God 217
- Day 4: Worship Through Songs 217
- Day 5: Serving Others With Joy 218
- Day 6: I'm Safe and Accepted in My Community 219
- Day 7: End-Of-Week Review 219

WEEK 32: SHARING THE GOSPEL: TELLING OTHERS ABOUT JESUS 221
- Day 1: The Gospel 221
- Day 2: Shining My Light 222
- Day 3: Sharing the Teachings of Jesus 223
- Day 4: Jesus' Love Is Unconditional 223
- Day 5: Declaring God's Glory 224
- Day 6: Inviting Others to Learn About Jesus 225
- Day 7: End-Of-Week Review 225

WEEK 33: THE BEATITUDES: LIVING THE BLESSED LIFE 227
- Day 1: The Beatitudes 227
- Day 2: Comforting Others 228
- Day 3: Being Gentle and Kind 228
- Day 4: Doing What's Right 229
- Day 5: Being Merciful 230
- Day 6: Being Peacemakers 231
- Day 7: End-Of-Week Review 231

WEEK 34: TRUST: RELYING ON GOD'S PROMISES 233
- Day 1: Confiding in God 233
- Day 2: Trusting God's Plans 234
- Day 3: God Is Truth 234
- Day 4: Relying On God 235
- Day 5: Being Safe in God 235
- Day 6: Being Brave and Courageous 236
- Day 7: End-Of-Week Review 237

WEEK 35: SPIRITUAL GIFTS: USING YOUR TALENTS FOR GOD 239
- Day 1: My Special Gifts 239
- Day 2: Growing My Gifts 240
- Day 3: Using My Gifts for Church 241
- Day 4: Sharing My Gifts to Help Others 241
- Day 5: Praising God for My Gifts 242
- Day 6: Developing My Gifts in God 243
- Day 7: End-Of-Week Review 243

WEEK 36: THE GOLDEN RULE: TREATING OTHERS THE WAY YOU WANT TO BE TREATED 245
- Day 1: What Is the Golden Rule? 245
- Day 2: Spreading Kindness 246
- Day 3: Practicing the Golden Rule 246
- Day 4: Helping Others 247
- Day 5: Apologizing 248
- Day 6: Practicing Active Listening 249
- Day 7: End-Of-Week Review 249

WEEK 37: THANKFULNESS: RECOGNIZING GOD'S GIFTS 251
- Day 1: What Is Thankfulness? 251
- Day 2: The Goodness of God 252
- Day 3: Filling My Heart With Joy 252
- Day 4: Being Grateful for Others 253
- Day 5: Building Stronger Bonds 254
- Day 6: Faith and Thankfulness 255
- Day 7: End-Of-Week Review 255

WEEK 38: LIGHT IN THE DARKNESS: BEING A BEACON OF HOPE 257
- Day 1: Shining God's Love 257
- Day 2: Bringing Hope 258
- Day 3: Following the Light of Jesus 259

- Day 4: Being Chosen by God 259
- Day 5: Being a Light 260
- Day 6: Carrying God's Light 261
- Day 7: End-Of- Week Review 262

WEEK 39: ENDURANCE: STAYING STRONG IN TRIALS 263

- Day 1: What Is Endurance? 263
- Day 2: Growing Stronger Through Challenges 264
- Day 3: Trusting God 265
- Day 4: Thanking God for Your Victories 265
- Day 5: God's Promises 266
- Day 6: Finding Rest in God 267
- Day 7: End-Of-Week Review 268

WEEK 40: SACRIFICE: UNDERSTANDING GIVING YOUR BEST 269

- Day 1: What Is Sacrifice? 269
- Day 2: Making Sacrifices 270
- Day 3: Worshipping God Through Sacrifices 271
- Day 4: Being Humble 272
- Day 5: True Love 272
- Day 6: God Provides All I Need 273
- Day 7: End-Of-Week Review 274

WEEK 41: ETERNITY: THE PROMISE OF HEAVEN 275

- Day 1: The Gift of Heaven 275
- Day 2: Our Hope in Heaven 276
- Day 3: Living for Eternity 277
- Day 4: Celebrating God's Promise 277
- Day 5: Faith Journey 278
- Day 6: Sharing the Good News 279
- Day 7: End-Of-Week Review 280

WEEK 42: BOLDNESS: SHARING YOUR FAITH WITHOUT FEAR 281

- Day 1: Being Brave for Jesus 281
- Day 2: Trusting God's Strength 282
- Day 3: Sharing With Friends 283
- Day 4: Speaking Up for What Is Right 283
- Day 5: Sharing the Good News 284
- Day 6: Overcoming Fear 285
- Day 7: Celebrating Boldness 286

WEEK 43: THE POWER OF WORDS: SPEAKING LIFE AND TRUTH 287

- Day 1: Words Matter 287
- Day 2: Kind Words 288
- Day 3: Truth in Our Words 289
- Day 4: Words of Wisdom 290
- Day 5: Praying With Our Words 290
- Day 6: Words that Bless 291
- Day 7: Reflecting on Our Words 292

WEEK 44: RIGHTEOUSNESS: CHOOSING TO DO WHAT IS RIGHT 293

- DAY 1: WHAT IS RIGHTEOUSNESS? 293
- DAY 2: STANDING UP FOR WHAT IS RIGHT 294
- DAY 3: MAKING GOOD CHOICES 295
- DAY 3: STANDING UP FOR WHAT IS RIGHT 295
- DAY 4: HELPING OTHERS CHOOSE RIGHT 296
- DAY 5: RIGHTEOUS ACTIONS 297
- DAY 6: REFLECTING ON OUR CHOICES 298
- DAY 7: END-OF-WEEK REVIEW 299

WEEK 45: REPENTANCE: TURNING AWAY FROM WRONG 301

- DAY 1: UNDERSTANDING REPENTANCE 301
- DAY 2: GOD'S" FORGIVENESS 302
- DAY 3: MAKING AMENDS 303
- DAY 4: TURNING AWAY FROM TEMPTATION 303
- DAY 5: THE JOY OF REPENTANCE 304
- DAY 6: LEARNING FROM MISTAKES 305
- DAY 7: CELEBRATING FORGIVENESS 306

WEEK 46: THE IMPORTANCE OF FAMILY: HONORING AND RESPECTING FAMILY 307

- DAY 1: GOD'S GIFT OF FAMILY 307
- DAY 2: HONORING PARENTS 308
- DAY 3: HELPING FAMILY MEMBERS 309
- DAY 4: FAMILY TIME 309
- DAY 5: LISTENING TO EACH OTHER 310
- DAY 6: FAMILY TRADITIONS 311
- DAY 7: END-OF-WEEK REVIEW 312

WEEK 47: GUIDANCE: SEEKING GOD'S DIRECTION 313

- DAY 1: LISTENING TO GOD 313
- DAY 2: PRAYING FOR DIRECTION 314
- DAY 3: TRUSTING IN GOD'S PLAN 314
- DAY 4: READING SCRIPTURE FOR WISDOM 315
- DAY 5: FOLLOWING GOD'S PATH 316
- DAY 6: SEEKING HELP FROM OTHERS 317
- DAY 7: END-OF-WEEK REVIEW 317

WEEK 48: UNITY: WORKING TOGETHER IN LOVE 319

- DAY 1: THE POWER OF TOGETHERNESS 319
- DAY 2: HELPING ONE ANOTHER 320
- DAY 3: SPEAKING KIND WORDS 320
- DAY 4: WORKING ON A TEAM 321
- DAY 5: ACCEPTING DIFFERENCES 322
- DAY 6: PRAYING FOR UNITY 323
- DAY 7: END-OF-WEEK REVIEW 323

WEEK 49: REDEMPTION: THE POWER OF A SECOND CHANCE 325

- DAY 1: UNDERSTANDING REDEMPTION 325
- DAY 2: LEARNING FROM MISTAKES 326

- Day 3: Forgiving Others 327
- Day 4: Accepting God's" Forgiveness 327
- Day 5: Sharing the Message of Redemption 328
- Day 6: The Joy of a Second Chance 329
- Day 7: Reflecting on Redemption 330

WEEK 50: THE FRUIT OF THE SPIRIT: LIVING WITH GODLY QUALITIES 331

- Day 1: What Is the Fruit of the Spirit? 331
- Day 2: The Importance of Love 332
- Day 3: Experiencing Joy 333
- Day 4: Practicing Peace 334
- Day 5: Kindness Matters 334
- Day 6: Being Gentle 335
- Day 7: Celebrating the Fruit of the Spirit 336

WEEK 51: THE GOOD SHEPHERD: JESUS' CARE FOR US 339

- Day 1: Who Is the Good Shepherd? 339
- Day 2: Trusting Jesus' Guidance 340
- Day 3: Jesus Protects Us 341
- Day 4: Finding Comfort in Jesus 341
- Day 5: Caring for Others 342
- Day 6: Following the Shepherd's Voice 343
- Day 7: End-Of-Week Review 344

WEEK 52: COMMISSION: SHARING GOD'S MESSAGE WORLDWIDE 345

- Day 1: What Is the Great Commission? 345
- Day 2: Telling Friends About Jesus 346
- Day 3: Serving Others in Love 347
- Day 4: Praying for the World 347
- Day 5: Living Out the Great Commission 348
- Day 6: Sharing Faith Stories 349
- Day 7: End-Of-Week Review 350

CONCLUSION 351

REFERENCES 353

Introduction

Hey there! Welcome to a super fun and exciting journey that's all about discovering faith, exploring spirituality, and having loads of fun along the way.

Why is this book so special, you might ask? Great question! This devotional is packed with cool activities and meaningful lessons designed especially for kids just like you. Imagine having a blast while learning about important topics like kindness, gratitude, and bravery—all from a spiritual angle. And guess what? You're not going on this adventure alone because your family can join in, too!

Each week, we'll dive into different themes and stories that come straight from scripture. These aren't just any old stories—they're tales that will spark your imagination and help you think about your own life in new ways. Plus, we have affirmations and prayers that are easy to understand and relate to, making it simple to connect with your faith every day.

Now, let's get into how this journey can involve your whole family. Imagine sitting together with your parents or siblings, reading through a story, and then talking about how it relates to your own lives. How awesome would it be to create something like a "Creation Collage" together, where everyone shares their favorite things about God's world? Not only will you learn a lot, but you'll also make some amazing memories.

As you go through each week, you're going to find yourself looking forward to the next day's activity. Some days, you might read a story that makes you think, *Whoa, I never thought of it that way!* Other days, you might do an activity that's so much fun you forget you're actually learning something important. And the best part? You can revisit your favorite sections anytime you want. It's like having your own little library of wisdom right at your fingertips.

So, what do you need to get started? You need only some time each day, an open heart, and maybe a little curiosity. Whether you read in the morning to start your day on a positive note or before bed to reflect on everything you did, this devotional fits perfectly into your routine.

So, grab your book, gather your loved ones, and let's start this incredible journey together! Whether you're creating art, sharing stories, or diving deep into thoughtful discussions, every moment spent with this book will be a step toward a brighter, more fulfilled life. Let the adventure begin!

Before You Start

How to Practice Meditation?

On some days of this 52-week devotional and affirmations book, you'll be encouraged to meditate. This practice helps to calm the mind and connect with God through silence and stillness. To embark on this exciting journey, carefully follow these steps:

1. Find a quiet and comfortable place to sit or lie down. Find a calm setting where you can focus.
2. Close your eyes gently and take a deep breath in through your nose. This helps your mind relax.
3. Hold your breath for a moment, then slowly breathe out through your mouth.
4. Focus on your breathing, noticing how your chest rises and falls. Keep breathing in and breathing out.
5. If your mind starts to wander, gently bring your attention back to your breath. It can be tricky to silence your thoughts. But don't worry, with practice, you'll get better at it.
6. Continue breathing deeply and quietly for a few minutes. It can be 5 or 10 minutes. The important thing is to be consistent and patient with yourself.
7. When you're ready, slowly open your eyes and notice how you feel.
8. Take a moment to appreciate the calmness before getting up.

Prayer and Devotion

When you pray, it's important to find a quiet space where you can focus without distractions. Once you're settled, take some deep breaths to calm your mind before starting your prayers. To do so, inhale through your nose and slowly exhale through your mouth.

When you pray, it's essential to express your thankfulness to God. You can voice your appreciation for how good your day was or how healthy you feel. When you start your prayer with gratitude, you feel connected to God and instill joy in yourself. Additionally, it's crucial to create a routine that includes prayer and devotion at a specific time each day by following the prayers and devotions scheduled in this book.

Journaling

Journaling is the art of writing your thoughts and feelings. It encourages your mind to reflect on God and yourself. When you practice journaling, it's vital to get prepared. Here's how to do it:

1. Find a notebook or journal you like and can use to write your thoughts and feelings. Whenever you pick up this book, make sure to have your journal within your reach.
2. Choose a quiet and comfortable spot to write where you can focus without distractions. It's also important to find the right time of the day when you aren't busy with other tasks.
3. Start with a fun title for your journal entry, like "My Day," "What I Learned," or the daily theme suggested in this book. You can find these at the top of each page.
4. Write the date at the top of the page so you can remember when you wrote it.
5. Begin by writing a few sentences about your thoughts when you read this book.
6. Don't forget to share your feelings about what you're reading.
7. Reflect on what you learned from today's devotion and your plans for the future.
8. Draw a picture or doodle if you want to express your thoughts in a creative way.
9. Read over your entry and think about what you wrote. This helps deepen your understanding of your feelings and experiences.
10. Close your journal and keep it safe; you can always come back and read what you've written later.

Week 1: God's Amazing World

Day 1: The Beginning of Everything

Devotion

God created the world from nothing by simply speaking. His words hold power, and He created everything around us.

Once upon a time, before anything existed, there was only a big, endless emptiness. In this emptiness lived God, who was full of love and imagination. One day, God decided it was time to create a magnificent world with His powerful words!

"Let there be light!" God said, and just like that, a bright light burst into the darkness. God smiled and called the light "Day," while the darkness became "Night."

Next, God looked around and said, "Let there be a sky above and waters below!" Suddenly, a beautiful blue sky stretched wide, and fluffy white clouds floated gently above. Below the sky, waters filled with waves danced together, sparkling like diamonds.

"Now, let the land appear!" God said, and the ground began to rise into mountains, valleys, and hills. The colorful plants and flowers sprouted from the earth, swaying in the gentle breeze.

Then, God said, "Let's fill the skies with birds and the waters with fish!" Suddenly, birds of every color chirped joyfully as they flew high, and all kinds of fish splashed merrily in the oceans and rivers.

But God wasn't finished yet! "Let us create animals of all kinds," He declared. And just like that, playful puppies, majestic lions, silly monkeys, and gentle elephants filled the land.

Finally, God said, "Let us create people!" And from the earth, God shaped Adam and Eve, the first humans.

When everything was created, God looked at the world and said, "This is very good!" He rested on the seventh day, enjoying the beauty of His creation.

And so, the world—filled with light, land, skies, and wonderful creatures—became a joyful place for everyone.

Scripture

Genesis 1:1-2: "In the beginning, God created the heavens and the earth" (*Holy Bible NIV: New International Version*, n.d.).

Activity: Reflection

Spend 10 minutes in silence, thinking about the world around you. Write down three things you love about creation.

1. _____

2. _____

3. _____

Day 2: Light and Darkness

Light is essential for life. It helps plants grow, brings warmth, and lets us see everything around us. Each morning, the sun would rise, casting a bright glow across the earth.

Reflection

How does the beauty of a sunset or sunrise remind you of God's presence in your life?

_____

_____

_____

_____

_____

_____

Scripture

Genesis 1:3-4: "And God said, 'Let there be light,' and there was light" (*Holy Bible NIV: New International Version*, n.d.).

Affirmation

"I will be a light in the world, just as God is my light!"

Activity: Drawing

Draw a picture of your favorite light source (the sun, a lamp, or even a candle) and how it brightens your life.

Day 3: The Sky and the Waters

Scripture

Genesis 1:6-8: "And God said, 'Let there be a vault between the waters to separate water from water'" (*Holy Bible NIV: New International Version.*, n.d.).

Discussion

Why do you think God created the sky and waters? What purpose do they serve in our lives?

Activity: Listening

Find a quiet place outdoors. Close your eyes and listen to the sounds around you (wind, birds, water). What do you hear?

_____

_____

_____

_____

_____

_____

_____

Day 4: Land and Plants

Scripture

Genesis 1:9-11: "Then God said, 'Let the water under the sky be gathered to one place, and let dry ground appear'" (*Holy Bible NIV: New International Version*, n.d.).

Prayer

Dear God,

Thank You for the plants and flowers so bright,

For the beauty they bring and the joy in our sight.

Help us to take care of the earth, every day,

To cherish Your creation in every little way,

In Your Holy Name,

Amen.

Activity: Journaling

Write about your favorite plant or flower. Describe what it looks like and why you love it.

_____

_____

_____

Day 5: The Sun, Moon, and Stars

God created the sun to brighten our days. The sun is a massive ball of gas that provides light and heat. It rises every morning, filling the world with warmth. Without the sun, life on Earth would not be possible.

Alongside the sun, God also created the moon. The moon shines in the night sky, providing a softer, gentler light. It reflects the sun's rays, glowing brightly against the dark backdrop of the night. The moon goes through different phases, such as the new moon, full moon, and crescent. Each phase brings its own unique beauty. For example, during a full moon, the night becomes almost as bright as day.

People often find themselves inspired by the moon's changing shape and brightness. Lastly, God scattered the stars across the heavens, designing constellations that would tell stories and guide travelers. Some burned fiercely, while others shimmered softly. As the stars took their places, they became symbols of hope, signs of seasons, and reminders of the vastness of the universe.

Journaling

Write about your favorite time of day—morning, afternoon, or evening. How does the sun, moon, or stars make that time special for you?

Scripture

Genesis 1:14-16: "And God said, 'Let there be lights in the vault of the sky to separate the day from the night'" (*Holy Bible NIV: New International Version*, n.d.).

Activity: Drawing

Illustrate a beautiful sunrise or sunset. Show the colors of the sky, the setting or rising sun, and how it affects the landscape around it.

Day 6: Creatures of the Sea and Sky

Scripture

Genesis 1:20-21: "And God said, 'Let the water teem with living creatures, and let birds fly above the earth'" (*Holy Bible NIV: New International Version*, n.d.).

Affirmation

"I love the animals God created and will show them kindness."

Activity: Challenge

Visit a local park or aquarium, or research a sea creature or bird online. Learn one new fact and share it with a family member.

Day 7: End-Of-Week Review

- **Recap:** Discuss with your family what you've learned about God's creation this week.
- **Reflection:** Genesis 1:26-27: "Then God said, 'Let us make mankind in our image, in our likeness...'" (*Holy Bible NIV: New International Version*, n.d.).
- **Family Activity:** Each member of the family writes down three things they love about themselves that reflect God's creation. Then, each takes a turn and shares them with others.
- **Preparation for Next Week:** Just like how we trust our parents or friends to take care of us, we can trust God to be there for us no matter what happens.

Week 2: Faith: Trusting God in Everything

Day 1: What Is Faith?

Devotion

Faith is believing in God even when we can't see Him.

Once upon a time, in a land long ago, there lived a man named Abraham. He was a kind and faithful person who loved God with all his heart. One day, God spoke to Abraham and made him a special promise.

"Abraham," God said, "I will make you the father of a great nation, and your descendants will be as numerous as the stars in the sky!"

Even though he couldn't see the promise right in front of him, Abraham began to trust God completely. He believed that God would keep His word, even when it seemed impossible. Every night, Abraham would go outside and look up at the stars. He would remember God's promise and smile.

God sent a message to them. "You will have a son, and his name will be Isaac!"

Abraham and Sarah couldn't believe it. They laughed with joy, but they also felt nervous. Yet, they chose to have faith in God. And just as God promised, many months later, Isaac was born! Their hearts were filled with happiness, and they named him Isaac, which means "laughter."

Through their faith and trust in God, Abraham and Sarah saw that God was always working behind the scenes, even when they couldn't see how things would happen.

Scripture

Hebrews 11:1: "Now faith is confidence in what we hope for and assurance about what we do not see" (*Holy Bible NIV: New International Version*, n.d.).

Activity: Reflection

Think about a time when you had to trust someone. Write about it in your journal.

Day 2: Faith in Action

Reflection

In your opinion, why is it important to have faith in God, especially in a world full of uncertainty?

_____

_____

_____

_____

_____

_____

_____

Scripture

James 2:17: "In the same way, faith by itself, if it is not accompanied by action, is dead" (*Holy Bible NIV: New International Version*, n.d.).

Affirmation

"My faith leads me to take action!"

Activity: Scripture Exploration

Read the story of Noah (Genesis 6-9). Discuss how Noah trusted God to build the ark.

Day 3: Trusting God in Tough Times

Scripture

Proverbs 3:5-6: "Trust in the Lord with all your heart and lean not on your own understanding" (*Holy Bible NIV: New International Version*, n.d.).

Discussion

How does talking about our struggles with others help us trust God more? Can sharing our burdens with friends or family make a difference?

Activity: Challenge

Think of one thing that makes you uncomfortable (like speaking in front of others or trying a new activity) and take a small step toward facing that fear while trusting God for strength.

Day 4: God's" Promises

Scripture

2 Peter 1:4: "Through these, he has given us his very great and precious promises" (*Holy Bible NIV: New International Version*, n.d.).

Prayer

Dear God,

Thank You for Your incredible promises that bring hope and joy to our hearts. Thank You for the blessings You have given us and for the plans You have for our lives.

Help us, Lord, to remember Your promises in times of doubt and uncertainty. Fill our hearts with Your love and peace, so that we may always trust in Your plans.

In Jesus' name, we pray,

Amen.

Meditation

Picture yourself sitting in a beautiful garden filled with vibrant flowers. Each flower represents one of God's promises. Feel the warmth of God's presence surrounding you.

Activity: Faith-Based Game

Play a game called "Promise Ball." Toss a ball to friends, and whoever catches it must share a promise of God.

Day 5: Helping Others Trust God

One way to show our faith is by being reliable. When we commit to helping others, we must follow through on our promises. For instance, if we agree to help a neighbor with their groceries, it is essential that we show up and do what we said we would. This reliability demonstrates that we care and that our faith encourages us to support one another. People appreciate when others keep their word. This simple act of fulfilling commitments can create an environment of trust and faith.

Journaling Prompts

Write down 10 reasons why helping others trust God can strengthen your own faith.

1. _____
2. _____
3. _____
4. _____
5. _____
6. _____
7. _____

8. _____

9. _____

10. _____

Scripture

Philippians 2:4: "Not looking to your own interests but each of you to the interests of the others" (*Holy Bible NIV: New International Version*, n.d.).

Activity: Drawing

Draw your own hands and fill each finger with ways you can pray for and support others in trusting God.

Day 6: Faith Like a Child

Scripture

Matthew 18:3: "Truly I tell you, unless you change and become like little children, you will never enter the kingdom of heaven" (*Holy Bible NIV: New International Version*, n.d.).

Affirmation

"My faith is simple and strong."

Activity: Reflection

Write down the list of things or people you trust God for, like your family or a dream.

_____

_____

_____

_____

_____

_____

_____

Day 7: End-Of-Week Review

- **Discussion:** Discuss with your friends what you've learned about the power of faith this week.
- **Reflection:** Mark 16:15: "Go into all the world and preach the gospel to all creation" (*Holy Bible NIV: New International Version*, n.d.).
- **Family Activity:** Share with your family how God has helped you trust Him.
- **Preparation for Next Week:** Imagine having a special friend who listens to you no matter where you are—at the playground, in your room, or even on a family trip! That's what prayer is all about: talking to God anywhere and anytime about anything on your heart.

Week 3: Prayer: Talking to God Anywhere

Day 1: What Is Prayer?

Devotion

Prayer is simply talking to God, just like talking to a friend.

One day, while Samuel was tending to the sheep, he sat down under a big tree to rest. He looked up at the sky and thought, "God is the powerful creator of the Universe, but He always finds ways to take care of me!"" Samuel decided that he wanted to talk to God just like he would talk to his best friend. So, he closed his eyes and began sharing his thoughts.

"Dear God," he prayed with a smile, "thank You for the sunny day and for the wonderful friends I have. I hope Grandma feels better. Please keep her safe!" After talking, Samuel opened his eyes and felt happy inside, as if he had just shared a secret with a close friend.

That evening, as Samuel lay in bed, he told God about his hopes and dreams, just like he would tell his mother or friends. Samuel understood that prayer wasn't just for special times; it could happen anywhere—while walking, playing, or even sitting quietly.

The next day, Samuel's mother noticed he was talking to God often. "Samuel," she said with a smile, "prayer is simply talking to God, just like talking to a friend. You can tell Him anything!"

And so, Samuel learned the special power of prayer, understanding that talking to God was just like sharing life with a dear friend.

Scripture

1 Thessalonians 5:17: "Pray without ceasing" (*Holy Bible NIV: New International Version*, n.d.).

Activity: Reflection

Think about the last time you talked to God. Write it down in your journal.

Day 2: Types of Prayer

Reflection

What specific words or phrases do you often use in your prayers, and what significance do they hold for you?

_____

_____

_____

_____

_____

_____

_____

Scripture

Matthew 6:9-13 (The Lord's Prayer): "Our Father in heaven, hallowed be your name, your kingdom come, your will be done, on earth as it is in heaven. Give us today our daily bread. And forgive us our debts, as we also have forgiven our debtors. And lead us not into temptation, but deliver us from the evil one" (*Holy Bible NIV: New International Version*, n.d.).

Affirmation

"I can pray in many ways!"

Activity: Scripture Exploration

Read and discuss the Lord's Prayer. What does each part mean?

Day 3: Prayer Warriors

Scripture

James 5:16: "The prayer of a righteous person is powerful and effective" (*Holy Bible NIV: New International Version*, n.d.).

Discussion

What does being a prayer warrior mean to you? Can you share a story of a time when you felt your prayers made a difference in someone else's life?

Challenge

Commit to praying for a specific person or group of people in need each day for 30 days. Keep a journal to track prayers and any updates on their situations.

Day 4: Listening to God

Scripture

Psalm 46:10: "Be still, and know that I am God" (*Holy Bible NIV: New International Version*, n.d.).

Prayer

Dear God,

I come before You with a humble heart, seeking Your guidance and peace. In the midst of my busy life, help me to be still and quiet my thoughts. Teach me to listen for Your voice amid the noise and distractions around me.

Help me to trust in Your timing and to find solace in the moments of stillness. Thank You for Your love and the promise that You are always with me.

Amen.

Meditation

Spend a few minutes quietly listening for God's voice. Write down any thoughts you receive.

Activity: Drawing

Create a large drawing of ears surrounded by elements that represent God's voice, such as birds, gentle whispers, or flowing water, with a child sitting quietly nearby, symbolizing their readiness to listen.

Day 5: Thankful Prayers

Thankfulness helps us recognize God's goodness. Taking a moment to think about what we are thankful for can change our perspective. For example, consider the simple act of waking up each day. Many people take this for granted, but waking up is a blessing. When we incorporate this into our prayers, it reinforces our awareness of the many gifts we receive. When we acknowledge God's goodness, it can be freeing. It allows us to release worries or negative feelings we might be holding onto.

Journaling

Write down three things you are thankful for and pray about them.

1. _____
2. _____
3. _____

Activity: Drawing

Draw a rainbow, with each color representing a different reason to be thankful.

Day 6: Praying Together

Scripture

Matthew 18:20: "For where two or three gather in my name, there am I with them" (Holy Bible NIV: New International Version, n.d.).

Affirmation

"I love praying with others!"

Activity: Challenge

Get together with family or friends and pray together for each other's needs.

Day 7: End-Of-Week Review

- **Discussion:** Discuss with your family all the insights you've learned about praying and listening to God.
- **Reflection:** Colossians 4:2: "Devote yourselves to prayer, being watchful and thankful" (*Holy Bible NIV: New International Version*, n.d.).
- **Family Activity:** Create a prayer jar where family members can write down prayer requests on

slips of paper. Each week, take turns picking a slip from the jar and praying for that request together as a family.

- **Preparation for Next Week:** In Matthew 6:14-15, Jesus teaches that if we forgive others for their trespasses, our Heavenly Father will forgive us.

Week 4: Forgiveness: Letting Go of Grudges

Day 1: Understanding Forgiveness

Devotion

Forgiveness means letting go of hurt and choosing to forgive others.

In a distant land, there was a caring father with two sons. The younger son, Luke, loved adventure and wanted to explore the world. One day, Luke asked his father for his share of the inheritance so he could go on his own journey. The father, who loved Luke very much, gave him the money.

Luke packed his things, said goodbye, and went to a new city. He spent his money on nice clothes, good food, and many parties. Soon, he ran out of money and found himself alone. Feeling worried and hungry, Luke realized he had made a mistake. He thought about his kind father. "Maybe I can go back and ask him to forgive me. I can say I'm sorry and promise to work hard," Luke decided.

As he walked home, he felt nervous about how his father would react. But when his father saw him from a distance, he was filled with joy and ran to hug him. "Luke! My son! I'm thrilled you're home!" The father opened his arms wide to welcome him back. Luke said, "Father, I have done wrong and don't deserve to be called your son." But the father smiled and said, "You are my son! Let's celebrate! You were lost, and now you're found!"

The father told his servants to prepare a feast. They cooked delicious food, played music, and invited everyone to join the celebration. The whole town was happy that Luke had returned. However, the older brother, Mark, was not pleased. When he heard the music and saw the party, he became angry. He told his father, "I've worked hard for you all these years, and you never threw me a party! Why are you celebrating Luke when he wasted your money?" The father gently replied, "My dear Mark, you have always been here, and everything I have is yours. We had to celebrate because your brother was lost and has come back to us. We must forgive him and be happy!"

Mark realized that forgiveness means letting go of pain and welcoming those who have made mistakes. He saw the love his father had for Luke and understood that everyone deserves a second chance. From then on, the brothers learned the importance of forgiveness and family. They enjoyed being together, knowing that love and forgiveness could mend even the deepest wounds.

Scripture

Ephesians 4:32: "Be kind and compassionate to one another, forgiving each other, just as in Christ God forgave you" (*Holy Bible NIV: New International Version*, n.d.).

Activity: Reflection

Think about someone you need to forgive. Write a short note expressing your feelings.

Day 2: Jesus Forgives Us

Reflection

Reflect on your own experience where you found it challenging to forgive someone. What steps can you take to follow Jesus' example of forgiveness in that situation?

_____

_____

_____

_____

_____

_____

_____

Scripture

Luke 23:34: "Jesus said, 'Father, forgive them, for they do not know what they are doing'" (*Holy Bible NIV: New International Version*, n.d.).

Affirmation

"I am forgiven by Jesus!"

Activity: Journaling

Write about a time when you felt forgiven. How did it feel?

_____

_____

_____

_____

_____

_____

_____

Day 3: The Importance of Forgiveness

Scripture

Matthew 6:14: "For if you forgive other people when they sin against you, your heavenly Father will also forgive you" (*Holy Bible NIV: New International Version*, n.d.).

Discussion

What does it truly mean to forgive someone, and how might this journey affect your connection to God?

Activity: Drawing

Create a "Forgiveness Tree." Draw a tree and write down the names of people you are forgiving on the leaves.

Day 4: Forgiving Ourselves

Scripture

1 John 1:9: "If we confess our sins, he is faithful and just and will forgive us our sins" (*Holy Bible NIV: New International Version*, n.d.).

Prayer

Dear God,

I come to You seeking strength and peace. Help me to forgive myself for my mistakes and to fully trust in Your forgiveness.

Teach me the ways to accept myself. Remind me that I am loved and valued, no matter my past. Guide me to learn and grow from my experiences.

In Jesus' Name,

Amen.

Meditation

Take a moment to think of something you struggle to forgive yourself for. Pray specifically about it.

Day 5: Acts of Kindness

Forgiveness can bring about positive changes in our lives and our relationships with others. It means letting go of anger and resentment toward someone who has hurt us. When we choose to forgive, we create space for healing and growth for ourselves and those around us. This process can transform our emotional state and improve our well-being.

When we practice forgiveness, we often find that it leads us to act more kindly toward others. For example, if someone has hurt us, we might feel angry or upset. This negativity can affect how we treat those around us. However, once we let go of those feelings through forgiveness, we become more open and compassionate. This shift in mindset can help us reach out, support, and be kind to others who may be struggling.

Journaling

Reflect on why you should always forgive your friends and family.

_____

_____

_____

_____

_____

_____

_____

Activity: Drawing

Draw a picture of two kids happily sharing their toys with each other at the playground.

Day 6: Letting Go of Grudges

Scripture

Proverbs 17:9: "Whoever would foster love covers over an offense" (*Holy Bible NIV: New International Version*, n.d.).

Affirmation

"I let go of grudges and choose love!"

Activity: Challenge

Write down any grudges you are holding onto. Pray over them and ask God to help you let them go.

_____

_____

_____

_____

_____

_____

_____

Day 7: End-Of-Week Review

- **Recap:** Discuss what you've learned from this week's topic: forgiveness.
- **Scripture:** Psalm 103:12: "As far as the east is from the west, so far has he removed our transgressions from us" (*Holy Bible NIV: New International Version*, n.d.).
- **Family Activity:** Watch a movie that highlights themes of forgiveness, such as *The Lion King* or *The Gruffalo*. Discuss the characters' decisions to forgive and what it meant for their relationships.
- **Preparation for Next Week:** We should always be kind to our surroundings. Kindness is pleasing God.

Week 5: Kindness: Making a Difference Every Day

Day 1: What Is Kindness?

Devotion

Kindness is treating others with love and respect, just as God loves us.

Long ago, in the land of Israel, Jesus traveled from town to town, teaching people about love, kindness, and how to live in harmony with one another. One day, as He spoke to a crowd, a curious lawyer stood up and asked, "Teacher, what must I do to inherit eternal life?"

Jesus replied, "What is written in the Law? How do you read it?"

The lawyer answered, "Love the Lord your God with all your heart, soul, and strength, and love your neighbor as yourself."

"You are right," said Jesus. "Do this, and you will live." But the lawyer wanted to justify himself, so he asked, "And who is my neighbor?"

To answer this question, Jesus told a story.

"A man was traveling from Jerusalem to Jericho when he was attacked by robbers. They stripped him of his clothes, beat him up, and left him half dead on the side of the road.

"A priest came along and saw the man, but he crossed to the other side of the road and walked right past him. Next, a Levite came to the spot, and he, too, saw the man but chose to pass by on the other side.

"Finally, a Samaritan came along. When he saw the man, he felt compassion for him. He went to him, bandaged his wounds, and poured oil and wine on them. Then he lifted the man onto his own donkey and took him to an inn, where he cared for him all night.

"The next day, the Samaritan paid the innkeeper and said, 'Take care of him. If his bill is higher, I will pay you back when I return.'"

After telling the story, Jesus looked at the lawyer and asked, "Which of these three do you think was a neighbor to the man who fell into the hands of robbers?"

The lawyer replied, "The one who had mercy on him."

Jesus smiled and said, "Go and do likewise."

Scripture

Ephesians 4:32: "Be kind and compassionate to one another" (*Holy Bible NIV: New International Version*, n.d.).

Activity: Reflection

Think about a time someone was kind to you. Write about how it made you feel.

_____

_____

_____

_____

_____

_____

_____

Day 2: The Kindness of Jesus

Reflection

Reflect on a time when you experienced kindness from someone during a difficult moment. How can that experience inspire you to extend kindness to those in need around you?

_____

_____

_____

_____

_____

_____

_____

Scripture

Luke 6:35: "Love your enemies, do good to them, and lend to them without expecting to get anything back" (*Holy Bible NIV: New International Version*, n.d.).

Affirmation

"I can show kindness just like Jesus!"

Activity: Reflection

Read the story of the Good Samaritan (Luke 10:25-37) and discuss how we can help others in need.

Day 3: Random Acts of Kindness

Scripture

Proverbs 11:17: "Those who are kind benefit themselves" (*Holy Bible NIV: New International Version*, n.d.).

Discussion

How does showing kindness to others boost the happiness and emotional health of the person being kind?

Activity: Challenge

Perform three random acts of kindness today. Keep track of what you did.

Day 4: Kindness in Our Words

Scripture

Proverbs 18:21: "The tongue has the power of life and death" (*Holy Bible NIV: New International Version*, n.d.).

Prayer

Dear God,

Give me the courage to speak words of hope and support to those who are feeling discouraged or down.

Help me to listen with compassion and respond with grace, understanding the struggles others may face.

Thank You for the gift of communication and the opportunity to make a difference in the lives of those around me.

In Your name, I pray,

Amen.

Activity: Journaling

Write down positive phrases or compliments you can say to others.

_____

_____

_____

_____

_____

_____

_____

Day 5: Sharing Kindness in Our Community

When we extend kindness to others, we create a ripple effect that can lead to a stronger, more connected society. Everyday acts of kindness are simple actions we can take to brighten someone's day. These can include holding the door open for a stranger, offering a compliment, or helping someone carry groceries. For example, if you see an elderly person struggling with heavy bags, you could stop and offer to help them. This small gesture could make a big difference in their day. These acts do not require a lot of time or effort, but they can have a significant impact.

Journaling

Kindness can extend beyond our families to our communities. Write down actions you can perform for them.

_____

_____

_____

_____

_____

_____

_____

Scripture

Galatians 6:10: "Therefore, as we have opportunity, let us do good to all people" (*Holy Bible NIV: New International Version*, n.d.).

Activity: Drawing

Draw three pictures of you performing acts of kindness for your community.

Day 6: The Ripple Effect of Kindness

Scripture

Matthew 5:16: "Let your light shine before others, that they may see your good deeds" (*Holy Bible NIV: New International Version*, n.d.).

Affirmation

"My kindness can inspire others!"

Activity: Art and Craft Project

Create a "Kindness Chain." Each link will represent an act of kindness done.

Day 7: End-Of-Week Review

- **Recap:** Discuss everything you've learned about kindness according to God's Words.
- **Scripture:** Galatians 5:22-23: "But the fruit of the Spirit is love, joy, peace, forbearance, kindness..." (*Holy Bible NIV: New International Version*, n.d.).

- **Family Activity:** Create a list of random acts of kindness (like holding the door open, leaving kind notes, or helping a neighbor) and challenge each other to complete as many as possible over a week.
- **Preparation for Next Week:** Gratitude is celebrating God's gifts. When you're grateful, you welcome them to your life.

Week 6: Gratitude: Thanking God for His Blessings

Day 1: What Is Gratitude?

Devotion

Gratitude is recognizing and appreciating the good things in our lives.

Once upon a time, there was a man who had a sickness called leprosy. This sickness made his skin sore and gave him terrible spots. Because of this, people were afraid to be near him, and he had to live far away from his family and friends. He felt very sad and lonely.

One sunny day, the man heard whispers in the air. "Did you hear? Jesus is coming to town!" He had heard amazing stories about Jesus—how He healed sick people and made sad hearts happy again. The man knew he had to find Jesus!

He ran to the road where Jesus was. He shouted, "Jesus! Please help me! Have mercy on me!"

When Jesus heard the man's voice, He stopped and turned. "What do you want me to do for you?" Jesus asked with kindness in His eyes.

"Please, Jesus! If you want to, you can make me clean. I want to be better!" The man said, his voice trembling with hope.

Jesus, filled with love and compassion, reached out His hand and touched the man. "I am willing. Be healed!" Instantly, the man felt the sickness leave him. His skin was clean and new, sparkling like the sun!

The man couldn't believe his eyes! He was healed! He jumped up and down with joy, shouting, "Thank You, Jesus! Thank You so much!"

But then, Jesus said, "Go and show yourself to the priest, and let him know you are healed." The man nodded excitedly and ran off to share the wonderful news.

As he hurried back to the town, he started to notice all the people he missed—his family, his friends, and even the flowers in the fields. His heart swelled with happiness. But as he celebrated with everyone, he realized something important: he hadn't gone back to thank the one person who had given him this amazing gift—Jesus!

So, the man turned around and ran back to find Jesus. When he found Him, he fell at Jesus' feet and said, "Thank You, Jesus! You healed me! I'm so grateful!"

Scripture

1 Thessalonians 5:18: "Give thanks in all circumstances" (*Holy Bible NIV: New International Version*, n.d.).

Activity: Reflection

Think about three things you are grateful for today and why. Write them down in your journal.

1. _____
2. _____
3. _____

Day 2: Counting Our Blessings

Reflection

Can you think of specific blessings in your life that may often go unnoticed?

_____
_____
_____
_____
_____
_____

Scripture

Psalm 100:4: "Enter his gates with thanksgiving and his courts with praise" (*Holy Bible NIV: New International Version*, n.d.).

Activity: Journaling

Start a gratitude journal and write down at least five blessings each day this week.

1. _____
2. _____
3. _____
4. _____
5. _____

Day 3: Thankfulness in Hard Times

Scripture

Romans 8:28: "And we know that in all things God works for the good of those who love him" (*Holy Bible NIV: New International Version*, n.d.).

Discussion

How does recognizing God's presence during tough times help us feel thankful, even when we encounter difficulties?

Activity: Challenge

Write about a difficult situation where you found something to be grateful for.

_____

_____

_____

_____

_____

_____

_____

Day 4: Gratitude in Prayer

Scripture

Philippians 4:6: "Do not be anxious about anything, but in every situation, by prayer and petition, with thanksgiving..." (*Holy Bible NIV: New International Version*, n.d.).

Prayer

Dear Lord,

I appreciate all that You do for me—Your countless blessings that often go unnoticed, Your guidance in times of uncertainty, and Your unwavering love that surrounds me every day.

Help me to remember always to come to You in prayer, sharing my thoughts, hopes, and fears. Teach me to recognize and appreciate Your work in my life, and inspire me to share that gratitude with others.

Lord, I am grateful for Your mercy, grace, and the assurance that I am never alone.

In your holy name, I pray,

Amen.

Activity: Challenge

Organize a small gathering where everyone shares something they are thankful for.

Day 5: Sharing Gratitude

When we share what we are thankful for, it can have a profound impact on those who hear us. For example, by telling a friend how much we appreciate their support during a tough time, our words can uplift them. And this can lead to a cycle of thankfulness. The person we thanked may feel encouraged to express their gratitude to someone else, creating a chain reaction of positive feelings. This sharing can lead to stronger relationships and a greater sense of community.

There are many ways to express gratitude: Writing thank you notes is a simple way to do so. These can be given to friends or family, showing them our appreciation. Also, taking a moment to write a few sincere sentences can make someone's day brighter. Additionally, we can express gratitude verbally. This could be as simple as saying "thank you" in everyday interactions or sharing how someone has positively impacted our lives.

Journaling

Write down 10 things you're grateful for this year.

1. _____
2. _____
3. _____
4. _____
5. _____
6. _____
7. _____
8. _____
9. _____
10. _____

Drawing

Create a thank-you card for God, expressing your thanks for the things He has done.

Activity: Sharing Opportunity

Share your drawing with your people.

Day 6: Thankfulness for Creation

Scripture

Psalm 104:24: "How many are your works, Lord! In wisdom you made them all; the earth is full of your creatures" (*Holy Bible NIV: New International Version*, n.d.).

Affirmation

"I thank God for His amazing creation!"

Activity: Art and Craft Project

Create a collage using nature items (leaves, flowers, etc.) and label it with things you are grateful for in creation.

Day 7: End-Of-Week Review

- **Recap:** Discuss how gratitude helps us focus on the positive in our lives.
- **Scripture:** Psalm 136:1: "Give thanks to the Lord, for he is good. His love endures forever" (*Holy Bible NIV: New International Version*, n.d.).
- **Family Activity:** Gather with your family and spend a day noticing and writing down every little thing each of you is thankful for.
- **Preparation for Next Week:** Accepting God's timing can be challenging. We often want things to happen according to our wishes and plans. Accepting that there is a bigger plan can be beneficial. This means trusting that God knows what is best for us, even if we do not see it at the moment.

Week 7: Patience: Waiting for God's Perfect Timing

Day 1: What Is Patience?

Devotion

Patience means waiting without getting upset. God teaches us to be patient.

Once upon a time, a boy named Joseph lived in a colorful land called Canaan. He was the favorite son of his father, Jacob, and he had a beautiful coat of many colors that his father had given him.

One night, Joseph had a special dream. In his dream, he saw himself and his brothers gathering bundles of grain in the fields. Suddenly, his brothers' bundles bowed down to his. Joseph was excited and told his brothers about the dream. But instead of being happy for him, they were very upset.

"Do you think you are better than us?" they shouted. "Will you rule over us?" Feeling hurt and angry, Joseph's brothers decided to get rid of him.

One day, when they were out in the fields, they plotted against him. They took Joseph's colorful coat and threw him into a deep pit. After that, they sold him to travelers going to a distant land. They told their father that a wild animal had eaten Joseph.

Joseph was taken to Egypt, far from his home and family. Joseph worked hard and eventually became trusted by Potiphar because everything he did was successful.

However, one day, something terrible happened. Potiphar's wife told lies about Joseph, and he was thrown into prison for a crime he did not commit. Now Joseph was alone again, but he didn't let anger or sadness take over his heart. He chose to be patient, even though it was very hard.

In prison, Joseph continued to trust God. He helped others by interpreting their dreams. He knew that God had a plan for him, and he waited patiently for that plan to unfold.

Scripture

James 1:4: "Let perseverance finish its work so that you may be mature and complete, not lacking anything" (*Holy Bible NIV: New International Version*, n.d.).

Activity: Reflection

Think about a time when you had to wait for something important. How did you feel? Write about it.

_____

_____

_____

_____

_____

_____

_____

Day 2: God's Timing Is Perfect

Scripture

Ecclesiastes 3:1: "There is a time for everything and a season for every activity under the heavens" (*Holy Bible NIV: New International Version*, n.d.).

Affirmation

"I trust that God's timing is the best."

Activity: Journaling

Write down something you are waiting for and ask God to help you be patient while you wait.

_____

_____

_____

_____

_____

_____

_____

_____

_____

Day 3: Waiting on God

Scripture

Psalm 27:14: "Wait for the Lord; be strong and take heart and wait for the Lord" (*Holy Bible NIV: New International Version*, n.d.).

Discussion

Why do you think waiting can be a good thing, and how does trusting God help us during those times?

Activity: Meditation

Spend a few minutes in quiet prayer, focusing on being still and waiting for God.

Day 4: The Rewards of Patience

Scripture

Galatians 6:9: "Let us not become weary in doing good, for at the proper time we will reap a harvest" (*Holy Bible NIV: New International Version*, n.d.).

Prayer

Dear Lord,

Help me to remember that patience brings rewards, especially when I face challenges and delays in my life. Teach me to trust in Your perfect timing and to embrace the lessons that come with waiting.

Thank You for the blessings that patience brings and for the growth it fosters within me. I trust that You have a plan for my life and that Your timing is always for my good.

In your name, I pray,

Amen.

Activity: Art and Craft Project

Create a "Patience Jar." Decorate the jar and write down situations where you need patience.

Day 5: Patience in Relationships

Showing patience with friends and family helps build strong relationships. It means giving them time to express themselves without rushing. When someone is upset or frustrated, waiting quietly can help them feel heard. For example, if a friend doesn't understand something in school, it's better to be calm and explain it again. This shows that you care about their feelings.

Being patient also means listening. Sometimes, people just want to talk about their day or share their worries. Instead of interrupting, it's good to let them finish what they are saying. This can make them feel important. When they feel valued, they are more likely to open up even more.

Journaling

Reflect on a time when you felt truly chosen and loved by God. How did that experience shape your understanding of compassion, kindness, humility, gentleness, and patience? Describe how you can embody these qualities in your daily life, especially in challenging situations.

_____

_____

_____

_____

_____

_____

_____

Drawing

Draw a serene landscape with a tranquil river flowing through it. Add a person sitting peacefully by the riverbank, practicing patience while observing nature. In the background, include gentle animals interacting kindly with each other, symbolizing harmony.

Activity: Sharing Opportunities

Plant seeds in small pots. As you wait for the plants to grow and care for them daily, share the importance of patience with your family.

Day 6: God's Waiting Room

Scripture

Isaiah 40:31: "But those who hope in the Lord will renew their strength. They will soar on wings like eagles" (*Holy Bible NIV: New International Version*, n.d.).

Affirmation

"I will trust in God while I wait."

Activity: Reflection

Spend time thinking about what God might be teaching you while you wait. Write it down.

_____

_____

_____

_____

_____

_____

_____

Day 7: End-of-Week Review

- **Recap:** Discuss and share with your family what you've learned from this week's topic: patience.
- **Scripture:** Philippians 4:6-7: "Do not be anxious about anything, but in every situation, by prayer and petition, with thanksgiving..." (*Holy Bible NIV: New International Version*, n.d.).
- **Family Activity:** Design a calendar together, assigning a specific act of kindness for each day of the month. Commit to completing those acts as a family.
- **Preparation for Next Week:** As we serve others, let's remember that the simple act of helping with a happy heart can lighten our hearts, brighten our spirits, and strengthen our communities.

Week 8: Serving Others: Helping With a Happy Heart

Day 1: The Call to Serve

Devotion

We are called to serve others just as Jesus served us.

Once upon a time, in a small village, there lived a kind and loving man named Jesus. He traveled from town to town, teaching everyone about love and kindness. The children loved to gather around him, listening with wide eyes as he shared stories.

One sunny day, Jesus noticed that his disciples were arguing over who was the greatest among them. They wanted to know who would sit next to him in heaven. Jesus listened quietly, then did something surprising. He took off his outer robe and filled a basin with water. His disciples looked at him curiously.

The disciples were shocked! "Lord, why are you washing our feet? You are our leader!" Peter exclaimed, not knowing what to say.

Jesus replied, "If I, your teacher, can wash your feet, then you should wash one another's feet. I have shown you this so that you can serve each other with love. This is how you show kindness."

The disciples were amazed. They realized that greatness in Jesus' eyes wasn't about being the best but about serving others and showing love. After Jesus finished, he said, "Go and do the same. Serve others just as I have served you."

Scripture

Mark 10:45: "For even the Son of Man did not come to be served, but to serve..." (*Holy Bible NIV: New International Version*, n.d.).

Activity: Reflection

Think about why it's important to serve others and write it in your journal.

Day 2: Kindness in Action

Reflection

How do you think serving others reflects your love for God and strengthens your relationship with Him?

Scripture

Galatians 5:13: "Serve one another humbly in love" (*Holy Bible NIV: New International Version*, n.d.).

Affirmation

"I will show love through my acts of service."

Activity: Drawing

Draw a picture of you helping someone or serving your community.

Day 3: Serving with a Happy Heart

Scripture

2 Corinthians 9:7: "God loves a cheerful giver" (*Holy Bible NIV: New International Version*, n.d.).

Discussion

How can we show joy and love when we help others, and why do you think it's important to serve from those feelings?

Activity: Challenge

Do something kind without expecting anything in return. Notice how it feels!

Day 4: Helping at Home

Scripture

1 Peter 4:10: "Each of you should use whatever gift you have received to serve others" (*Holy Bible NIV: New International Version*, n.d.).

Prayer

Dear Lord,

I come to You with a humble heart, asking for Your help in serving my family with love and joy.

Help me to embrace each moment spent with my family, finding joy in the small acts of service that can brighten their day. May my heart be filled with gratitude for the gift of family, and may I always strive to contribute positively to our relationships.

Thank You for the opportunity to serve and love those around me.

In your precious name, I pray,

Amen.

Activity: Service Project

Choose a chore or task to do for your family today without being asked.

Day 5: Serving in Our Community

Helping our community is a great way to make a difference in people's lives. When we think about lending a hand, it often comes from caring and understanding. People around us may face different problems, like not having enough money, health issues, or feeling lonely. By seeing these challenges, we can do something to support those who need it the most.

Journaling

Reflect on a time when you helped someone in need. What motivated you to take action, and how did it make you feel afterward?

_____

_____

_____

_____

_____

_____

_____

Scripture

Matthew 25:40: "Whatever you did for one of the least of these brothers and sisters of mine, you did for me" (*Holy Bible NIV: New International Version*, n.d.).

Prayer

"God, show me how I can help those in my community."

Activity: Art and Craft Project

Create cards for local nursing home residents or care packages for families in need.

Day 6: Teamwork in Service

Scripture

Ecclesiastes 4:9: "Two are better than one because they have a good return for their labor" (*Holy Bible NIV: New International Version*, n.d.).

Affirmation

"I enjoy serving others with my friends!"

Activity: Faith-Based Game

Organize a fun team activity that requires cooperation, like a group game or relay.

Day 7: End-Of-Week Review

- **Recap:** Discuss and share what you've learned from this week's topic with your family.
- **Scripture:** Colossians 3:23: "Whatever you do, work at it with all your heart, as working for the Lord" (*Holy Bible NIV: New International Version*, n.d.).
- **Family Activity:** Gather together as a family and take turns expressing gratitude for specific opportunities to serve others.
- **Preparation for Next Week:** In the hustle and bustle of everyday life, finding happiness in God's presence requires intentional moments of stillness and reflection. When we pause to seek Him through prayer and meditation on His word, we cultivate a deeper awareness of His love and grace enveloping us.

Week 9: Joy: Finding Happiness in God's Presence

Day 1: What Is Joy?

Devotion

Joy is a deep-seated happiness that comes from knowing God.

Once upon a time, in a bright and bustling village, there lived a little girl named Sarah. Sarah was cheerful and loved to play with her friends. They would run through the fields and laugh together, but sometimes Sarah noticed her friends felt sad or tired.

One day, while playing near a sparkling river, Sarah met an old woman sitting on a bench. The woman's face shone with a warm smile, and her eyes sparkled like the stars. Curious, Sarah approached her and asked, "Why are you so happy all the time?"

The old woman replied, "My dear, true joy comes from knowing God. It is a deep happiness that lives in your heart, no matter what is happening around you."

Sarah was puzzled. "How can you be joyful even when things are tough?" she asked.

The woman said, "Let me tell you a story. There once was a man named Paul. He traveled many places to share God's love. Sometimes, he faced hard times, like when he was thrown into prison. But even in that dark place, he sang songs of praise! He felt joy in his heart because he knew God was always with him."

"Really? What did he do?" Sarah inquired.

"He prayed and thanked God, knowing that God loved him and would help him through anything. That joy kept him strong, even in tough times," the woman explained.

Sarah thought about her own life. "I want to feel that kind of joy, too!" she exclaimed.

The woman smiled and said, "You can! Talk to God, thank Him for all the good things, and trust that He loves you. Joy will grow in your heart like the flowers in spring!"

Scripture

Philippians 4:4: "Rejoice in the Lord always. I will say it again: Rejoice" (*Holy Bible NIV: New International Version*, n.d.).

Activity: Reflection

Think about what brings you joy and write it in your journal.

_____

_____

_____

_____

_____

_____

_____

Day 2: Joy in Difficult Times

Reflection

Reflect on a challenging experience in your life where you discovered joy amidst the struggle. How did your faith contribute to that sense of joy, and what lessons did you learn that can help you in future tough times?

_____

_____

_____

_____

_____

Scripture

Nehemiah 8:10: "The joy of the Lord is your strength" (*Holy Bible NIV: New International Version*, n.d.).

Affirmation

"I can find joy even in difficult situations."

Activity: Challenge

When feeling sad, write down things that still bring you joy to remind yourself.

Day 3: Sharing Joy

Scripture

Psalm 126:2: "Our mouths were filled with laughter, our tongues with songs of joy" (*Holy Bible NIV: New International Version*, n.d.).

Discussion

How do you feel when you share something that makes you happy with your friends or family, and why do you think joy feels even greater when we share it?

Activity: Art and Craft Project

Create a "Joy Jar." Each time you experience joy, add a note to the jar.

Day 4: Joyful Praise

Scripture

Psalm 100:1: "Shout for joy to the Lord, all the earth" (*Holy Bible NIV: New International Version*, n.d.).

Prayer

Dear God,

Thank You for the ability to express my love and gratitude to You, and for the uplifting spirit that comes from sharing praises with others.

May my heart be open to celebrating Your blessings, both big and small, and may I find comfort and strength in my praise, especially during difficult times.

Thank You for the countless ways You bring happiness into my life and for the gift of being able to connect with You through worship.

In your loving name, I pray,

Amen.

Activity: Singing

Choose a worship song that makes you feel joyful and sing it out loud!

Day 5: Joy in Creation

The sky above is a large, colorful painting that changes every day. It can be bright blue in the morning, while at sunset, it lights up with orange and pink. At night, stars sparkle like tiny jewels, reminding us that we are not alone. Every part of nature ignites creativity and dreams, filling our hearts with excitement. Seasons also bring different joys. In winter, the world is covered in snow. Everyone loves the warmth in summer and heads to the beach to make sandcastles. Each season offers unique joys, helping us appreciate the variety of nature.

Nature teaches us valuable lessons about caring for the earth. When we notice its beauty, we become motivated to protect it. We learn that each of us is important in caring for the environment. Whether it's picking up trash or planting trees, every small effort counts. Every day presents new discoveries in the world, whether it's an unusual bug, a vibrant rainbow, or the gentle flutter of a bird's wings—beauty is everywhere.

Journal

What specific aspects of nature or moments in creation have brought you joy, and how can you make a habit of recognizing and appreciating those moments in your daily life?

_____

_____

_____

_____

_____

_____

_____

Scripture

Psalm 104:24: "How many are your works, Lord! In wisdom you made them all" (*Holy Bible NIV: New International Version*, n.d.).

Affirmation

"Lord, thank You for the beauty around me that brings me joy!"

Activity: Nature Walk

Go outside and take a walk, observing the beauty of nature. Write down what brings you joy in creation.

Day 6: Joy Through Gratitude

Scripture

1 Thessalonians 5:16-18: "Rejoice always, pray continually, give thanks in all circumstances..." (*Holy Bible NIV: New International Version*, n.d.).

Affirmation

"I will cultivate joy through gratitude!"

Activity: Journaling

Write down things you are thankful for and reflect on how they bring you joy.

_____

_____

_____

_____

_____

_____

_____

Day 7: End-Of-Week Review

- **Recap:** Discuss and share what you've learned from this week's topic with your family.
- **Scripture:** Acts 2:46: "They broke bread in their homes and ate together with glad and sincere hearts" (*Holy Bible NIV: New International Version*, n.d.).
- **Family Activity:** Plan a fun time with family or friends, focusing on joyful activities together.
- **Preparation for Next Week:** Peace is the profound calmness that God bestows upon our hearts, serving as a refuge during the tumultuous storms of life. In times of uncertainty, when the world around us feels chaotic, we can find solace in His presence, which transcends our understanding.

Week 10: Peace: Calm in the Storm

Day 1: What Is Peace?

Devotion

Peace is the calmness that God gives, even in difficult times.

A young boy named Seth lived in a small, peaceful village by the sea. Seth loved to explore the sandy beaches and watch the waves dance in the sunlight. However, there were days when dark clouds filled the sky, and strong winds shook the village. On those days, everyone felt anxious and worried.

One afternoon, as gray clouds gathered above, Seth's mother said, "Seth, let's go to the shore and pray for peace." Seth didn't fully understand what she meant but trusted his mother.

When they arrived at the beach, the waves crashed loudly against the rocks. Seth could feel the wind on his face. "Why are we here, Mom?" he asked.

His mother smiled softly and said, "We come to remind ourselves that even when storms come, God is always with us. Let's talk to Him."

They knelt on the cool sand, and Seth listened as his mother prayed for calmness and peace for everyone in the village. After they prayed, they sat quietly, feeling the wind and watching the waves.

Suddenly, Seth remembered a story his grandmother told him about Jesus. He thought about when Jesus was on a boat with his disciples, and a fierce storm arose. The waves were high, and the disciples were afraid. But Jesus was sleeping peacefully! When they woke him up, he simply said, "Peace! Be still!" And just like that, the storm stopped, and there was calm.

Feeling inspired, Seth whispered to his mother, "Just like Jesus, we can trust God to give us peace, even when things are scary!"

His mother nodded, "That's right, Seth! Peace is a gift from God. It's that calmness we feel in our hearts, even when we face difficult times."

As they watched the storm clouds slowly fade away, Seth closed his eyes, took a deep breath, and felt a warm sense of calm wash over him. He realized that God was with him, just like the sun hidden behind the clouds, waiting to shine again.

Scripture

John 14:27: "Peace I leave with you; my peace I give you" (*Holy Bible NIV: New International Version*, n.d.).

Activity: Reflection

Think about a time you felt God's peace and write about it.

_____

_____

_____

_____

_____

_____

_____

Day 2: Finding Peace in Prayer

Reflection

Have you experienced a significant sense of peace after praying or spending quiet time with God? What specific thoughts or feelings emerged during that time that you can carry into your daily life?

_____

_____

_____

_____

_____

_____

Scripture

Philippians 4:6-7: "Do not be anxious about anything, but in every situation, by prayer and petition, present your requests to God" (*Holy Bible NIV: New International Version*, n.d.).

Affirmation

"I find peace through prayer."

Activity: Meditation

Spend time in silent prayer, focusing on God and inviting His peace into your heart.

Day 3: Peace in Difficult Times

Scripture

Psalm 34:14: "Seek peace and pursue it" (*Holy Bible NIV: New International Version*, n.d.).

Discussion

How can we find peace in our hearts when we're feeling worried or scared, even if we're facing difficult situations?

Activity: Challenge

When you feel anxious, practice deep breathing and say a calming prayer.

Day 4: Sharing Peace With Others

Scripture

Matthew 5:9: "Blessed are the peacemakers, for they will be called children of God" (*Holy Bible NIV: New International Version*, n.d.).

Prayer

Dear Lord,

Help me to be a source of peace in every interaction I have. Give me the ability to listen with compassion, to speak with kindness, and to act with understanding.

May my actions reflect Your love and peace, creating a safe space for those I care about.

Thank You for the opportunity to make a difference in the lives of others.

In Your name, I pray,

Amen.

Activity: Service Project

Do something special for someone that encourages peace, like writing a kind note.

Day 5: Trusting God for Peace

God cares for us like a loving parent. We can talk to Him and share our feelings when we feel scared or worried. Just like how we might go to a friend when we're sad, going to God can help us feel better or even happier. We can ask God to help us with our problems, and we can trust that He is listening. It's easy to forget that we don't have to face everything alone. God wants to help us through tough times. When we turn to Him, we can feel the peace starting to grow in our hearts, helping us to smile again.

Besides, when we trust in God regularly, our hearts become stronger and steadier. Sometimes, things won't go the way we want, but that doesn't mean God isn't listening. He understands what we need even more than we do. By keeping our hearts open, we can discover the amazing ways He answers our prayers and supports us through everything.

Journaling

Write down things you trust God with to help cultivate peace in your heart.

_____

_____

_____

_____

_____

_____

_____

Scripture

Isaiah 26:3: "You will keep in perfect peace those whose minds are steadfast, because they trust in you." (*Holy Bible NIV: New International Version.*, n.d.)

Affirmation

"I trust God to give me peace."

Activity: Art and Craft Project

Create a "Trust Jar" where you write down your worries or fears on slips of paper and place them in the jar. Each time you add a new worry, take a moment to pray and surrender it to God, asking for His peace to fill your heart. Regularly revisit the jar to reflect on how God has brought peace into your life regarding those concerns.

Day 6: Peace in Nature

Scripture

Matthew 6:28-30: "See how the flowers of the field grow. They do not labor or spin" (*Holy Bible NIV: New International Version*, n.d.).

Affirmation

"I feel calm and peaceful in nature!"

Activity: Nature Walk

Take a peaceful walk outside. Reflect on the beauty around you, finding peace in creation.

Day 7: End-Of-Week Review

- **Recap:** Discuss and share what you've learned from this week's topic with your family.
- **Scripture:** Colossians 3:15: "Let the peace of Christ rule in your hearts" (*Holy Bible NIV: New International Version*, n.d.).

- **Family Activity:** With your family, write a list of things you appreciate in your life that bring you peace and share it with others.
- **Preparation for Next Week:** Hope nurtures resilience, allowing us to rise after every fall and embrace the unknown with courage and faith. By focusing on the possibility of brighter tomorrows, we cultivate a spirit that thrives amidst adversity, fueling our dreams and aspirations.

Week 11: Hope: Believing in Better Days

Day 1: What Is Hope?

Devotion

Hope is a confident expectation for the future.

A girl named Miriam lived in a lively little village surrounded by green hills. Miriam was known for her bright smile and cheerful spirit. She loved to help her neighbors and tell stories to the younger children about the wonderful things she dreamed of for the future.

One day, a terrible drought came to the village. The villagers worried, and some began to lose hope. They wondered how they would survive without water for their gardens and animals.

Miriam saw her friends and family looking sad and wanted to help. She remembered stories from the Bible about how God always provided for His people. One of her favorite stories was about a man named Noah, who built an ark because God promised to protect him from a great flood. He had hope that what God said would come true, even when no one else believed it.

With a heart full of faith, Miriam gathered everyone in the village. "Friends, let us not lose hope!" she encouraged. "Just like God provided for Noah, He will provide for us, too!"

Some villagers frowned and shook their heads. "But what if it doesn't rain? What will we do?" they asked.

Miriam smiled brightly and replied, "We can trust that God has a plan for us. Let's pray together and ask Him for rain!"

That evening, the villagers gathered in the main square. They held hands and prayed, asking God to send rain and to give them hope for the future. As they prayed, Miriam felt a strong sense of trust in her heart.

Days went by, and the skies remained clear and blue. Some villagers began to lose faith, but Miriam refused to give up. "I believe rain will come!" she said confidently.

Then, one bright morning, as Miriam was tending to her garden, she noticed a dark cloud forming in the sky. Her heart raced with excitement. She rushed to tell the others, "Look! The clouds are coming! God is answering our prayers!"

Sure enough, as the clouds gathered, the first drops of rain began to fall. The villagers cheered and danced with joy as the rain poured down, soaking the earth and bringing life back to their crops.

Miriam smiled and said, "This is just the beginning! We can always have hope because God keeps His promises!"

Scripture

Jeremiah 29:11: "For I know the plans I have for you, declares the Lord, plans to prosper you..." (*Holy Bible NIV: New International Version*, n.d.).

Activity: Reflection

Think about your hopes and dreams. Write them down in your journal.

_____

_____

_____

_____

_____

_____

_____

Day 2: Hope in God's Promises

Scripture

Romans 15:13: "May the God of hope fill you with all joy and peace as you trust in him" (*Holy Bible NIV: New International Version*, n.d.).

Affirmation

"I trust in God's promises."

Activity: Journaling

Write about a promise from God that gives you hope.

_____

_____

_____

_____

_____

_____

_____

Day 3: Hope in Difficult Times

Scripture

Psalm 39:7: "But now, Lord, what do I look for? My hope is in you" (*Holy Bible NIV: New International Version*, n.d.).

Discussion

What are some things we can do or think about to keep hope alive when we're going through tough times?

Activity: Prayer

When faced with a challenge, write a prayer asking God to help you hold onto hope.

Day 4: Sharing Hope With Others

Scripture

1 Peter 3:15: "Always be prepared to give an answer to everyone who asks you to give the reason for the hope that you have" (*Holy Bible NIV: New International Version*, n.d.).

Prayer

Dear God,

In a world that can often feel dark and discouraging, let me be a source of light and encouragement, bringing reassurance to those who are struggling.

Give me the courage to reach out and share words of hope and support, reminding them that they are not alone.

Thank You for the ability to spread hope, and may I always be willing to share the blessings You have given me.

In Your name, I pray,

Amen.

Activity: Art and Craft Project

Create a "Hope Wall" with notes of encouragement and hope that you can share with others.

Day 5: Hope Through Prayer

When friends or family pray, they share their feelings. They can talk about what makes them happy and what worries them. This helps everyone feel cared for. When they pray for each other, it shows love and support. Kids can pray for their friends, teachers, or pets. It can be a special way to connect and share hopes.

Finding hope and strength in prayer is a journey. Your experience with prayer will be unique, and that's special. It's a tool you can use throughout your life. Each prayer can lead to new thoughts, feelings, and understandings that enrich your hearts and minds.

Journaling

What are some specific prayers or moments of prayer that have provided you with hope and strength in your life?

_____

_____

_____

_____

_____

_____

_____

Scripture

Philippians 4:6-7: "In every situation, by prayer and petition, with thanksgiving, present your requests to God" (*Holy Bible NIV: New International Version*, n.d.).

Activity: Meditation

Spend quiet time in prayer, focusing on bringing your hopes to God.

Day 6: Hope in Community

Scripture

Hebrews 10:24-25: "And let us consider how we may spur one another on toward love and good deeds" (*Holy Bible NIV: New International Version*, n.d.).

Affirmation

"I find hope in my community."

Activity: Gathering

Plan a small gathering with friends or family to share stories of hope.

Day 7: End-Of-Week Review

- **Recap:** Discuss and share what you've learned from this week's topic with your family.
- **Scripture:** Jeremiah 17:7: "But blessed is the one who trusts in the Lord, whose confidence is in him." (*Holy Bible NIV: New International Version.*, n.d.)
- **Family Activity:** Gather the family for a gratitude night, where each member writes their own thank you note to God. Afterward, share these notes aloud, reflecting on the hope and strength each person feels in their lives. Consider decorating the notes to make them more personal and special.
- **Preparation for Next Week:** In a world that often challenges beliefs and moral principles, showing courage allows us to act in alignment with our convictions, building a deeper relationship with God.

Week 12: Courage: Standing Strong for God

Day 1: What Is Courage?

Devotion

Courage is doing what is right, even when it's hard.

Once upon a time, a young boy named David lived in a small village. David was not like many of the other children; he had a brave heart. He loved to care for his family's sheep in the fields, and every day, he would sing sweet songs to them.

One day, a fearsome giant named Goliath came to the land. He was tall and scary and wore heavy armor that made a loud clanking sound as he moved. Goliath challenged the soldiers of Israel to fight him, but no one dared to step forward. The soldiers were afraid and hid behind their shields.

When David heard about the giant, he felt a stirring in his heart. He knew Goliath was wrong for bullying the people of Israel, and he believed that someone had to stand up to him. Although David was just a shepherd boy and not a trained soldier, he gathered his courage and went to the king.

"King Saul," David said bravely, "I will fight Goliath. I will not let him scare us any longer!"

King Saul looked at David, surprised. "You are just a boy! Goliath is a mighty warrior. How can you possibly defeat him?"

David replied, "When a lion or a bear came to take one of my sheep, I fought them to protect my flock. God helped me then, and I trust He will help me now."

They dressed David in armor, but it was too heavy for him. Instead, David chose to wear his simple shepherd's clothes and took his slingshot and five smooth stones from the stream.

When David approached Goliath, the giant laughed. "Come here, little boy! I'll crush you!"

But David stood tall. "You come to me with a sword and spear, but I come to you in the name of the Lord! Today, He will help me defeat you!"

David placed a stone in his slingshot and aimed carefully. With a swift motion, he released the stone, and it flew straight toward Goliath. The stone hit the giant right in the forehead, and Goliath fell to the ground with a loud thud.

The people of Israel cheered! David had shown great courage by doing what was right, even when it was hard. From that day on, David became a hero, proving that bravery comes from God.

Scripture

Joshua 1:9: "Be strong and courageous. Do not be afraid; do not be discouraged, for the Lord your God will be with you wherever you go" (*Holy Bible NIV: New International Version*, n.d.).

Activity: Reflection

Think about a time when you had to be brave. Write about it.

_____

_____

_____

_____

_____

_____

_____

Day 2: Courage in Faith

Reflection

When facing a difficult situation, how can you actively remind yourself of God's presence and promises to inspire confidence and resilience in your heart?

_____

_____

_____

_____

_____

_____

_____

Scripture

2 Timothy 1:7: "For God has not given us a spirit of fear but of power, love, and a sound mind" (*Holy Bible NIV: New International Version*, n.d.).

Affirmation

"My faith gives me courage!"

Activity: Challenge

Face a small fear, like speaking up in class or trying something new, and share how you felt afterward.

Day 3: Courage to Stand Up for Others

Scripture

Proverbs 31:8: "Speak up for those who cannot speak for themselves" (*Holy Bible NIV: New International Version*, n.d.).

Discussion

Why do you think it's important to be brave and stand up for someone who is being treated unfairly, and how can we do that?

Activity: Faith-Based Game

Role-play different scenarios where you may need to stand up for someone and discuss how to handle them.

Day 4: The Courage of Daniel

Scripture

Daniel 3:16-18: "Shadrach, Meshach, and Abednego replied to him, 'King Nebuchadnezzar, we do not need to defend ourselves before you in this matter'" (*Holy Bible NIV: New International Version*, n.d.).

Prayer

Dear Lord,

Teach me to trust in You completely, knowing that You are always with me, guiding my path and supporting me in moments of fear or uncertainty.

May I be bold in sharing Your love and truth with others, reflecting Your light in a world that often needs it.

May I continually strive to follow You with courage and devotion.

In your name, I pray,

Amen.

Activity: Script Exploration

Read the story of Daniel in the lion's den (Daniel 6) and discuss Daniel's courage.

Day 5: Courage to Share Your Faith

Sharing our faith can feel scary sometimes. When we talk about what we believe, it might seem like we're taking a big step. Sometimes, we worry about what others might think. Will they laugh at us or not understand? It's normal to feel this way. Just like we might not like certain things, others might love what we share. Our faith can give them hope and guidance. If we stay quiet, they might never know the joy we feel.

We can start small. Talking to our friends at school is a good place to begin. We can tell them stories about how our faith helps us every day, as well as how we feel during tough times. Sharing how we feel during tough times can show them that faith is not just for Sundays; it's for every day.

Journaling

Write down one way you can share your faith with a friend or family member.

_____

_____

_____

_____

_____

_____

_____

Scripture

Matthew 10:32: "Whoever acknowledges me before others, I will also acknowledge before my Father in heaven" (*Holy Bible NIV: New International Version.*, n.d.).

Activity: Sharing Opportunity

Create a "Courage Cards" activity where you decorate small cards with messages about their faith, such as Bible verses, positive affirmations, or personal testimonies. Share them with your friends and family.

Day 6: Courage in Everyday Life

Scripture

Philippians 4:13: "I can do all this through him who gives me strength" (*Holy Bible NIV: New International Version*, n.d.).

Affirmation

"I am strong and can face anything!"

Activity: Challenge

Identify a small, everyday act of courage and do it, like trying a new activity.

Day 7: End-Of-Week Review

- **Recap:** Discuss and share what you've learned from this week's topic with your family.
- **Scripture:** Isaiah 41:10: "So do not fear, for I am with you; do not be dismayed, for I am your God" (*Holy Bible NIV: New International Version*, n.d.).
- **Family Activity:** Write a "Thank You" note to God, expressing your gratitude for the courage He provides.
- **Preparation for Next Week:** Speaking the truth in love is vital because it fosters authentic relationships built on trust and respect. By practicing honesty in a loving manner, we can guide one another toward positive change and growth.

Week 13: Honesty: Speaking the Truth in Love

Day 1: What Is Honesty?

Devotion

Honesty means being truthful and sincere with ourselves and others.

In the days of the Old Testament, there lived a shepherd named Nathan. He was known throughout his village for his kindness and honesty. People admired Nathan because he always spoke the truth and kept his promises.

One day, Nathan was tending to his sheep in the fields when he noticed a great noise coming from the nearby town. Curious, he set off to see what was happening. When he arrived, he found a large crowd gathered around the town square. They were listening to a man named Eli, who was known for his wisdom.

Eli spoke of a great king named David, who had an important message about being honest and truthful. As Nathan listened, he felt a stirring in his heart. He remembered a time when he had been tempted to tell a lie about losing some of his sheep. Instead of being truthful, he had thought about covering it up to avoid trouble.

That night, Nathan prayed for guidance and realized that honesty is not only about speaking the truth to others but also about being truthful with ourselves. He felt remorse for the moment he had chosen dishonesty over sincerity.

The next day, Nathan gathered the villagers and shared his experience. "Friends," he said, "I learned something important: Being honest means being truthful with ourselves and with each other. Just as King David leads with integrity, we must also lead with honesty. It strengthens our relationships and builds trust."

The villagers listened closely. Inspired by Nathan's words, they agreed to always speak the truth, no matter how difficult it might be. From that day forward, the village became known as a community of honesty where everyone felt free to share their thoughts and feelings sincerely.

Scripture

Ephesians 4:15: "Speaking the truth in love, we will grow to become in every respect the mature body of him who is the head, that is, Christ" (*Holy Bible NIV: New International Version*, n.d.).

Activity: Reflection

Think about a time when honesty was important to you. Write about it in your journal.

_____

_____

_____

_____

_____

_____

_____

Day 2: Honesty With Ourselves

Reflection

Reflect on a time when you struggled to acknowledge your true feelings or behaviors. What were the consequences, and how can embracing honesty improve your understanding of yourself and your interactions with others?

_____

_____

_____

_____

Scripture

Psalm 51:6: "You desire truth in the inward being." (*Holy Bible NIV: New International Version.*, n.d.)

Affirmation

"I will be truthful with myself."

Day 3: Honesty in Relationships

Scripture

Proverbs 12:22: "The Lord detests lying lips, but he delights in people who are trustworthy" (*Holy Bible NIV: New International Version.*, n.d.).

Discussion

How does being honest with our friends and family help us build stronger relationships, and why is trust important in those relationships?

Activity: Challenge

Practice sharing a true feeling with a friend or family member today.

Day 4: The Importance of Truth

Scripture

John 8:32: "Then you will know the truth, and the truth will set you free" (*Holy Bible NIV: New International Version*, n.d.).

Prayer

Dear Lord,

Help me to value honesty and integrity in all my thoughts, words, and actions. Teach me to recognize the power of truth and the freedom that comes from living authentically and transparently.

Guide me to seek Your truth above all else, even when it's difficult or inconvenient. May I always strive to represent You with sincerity, allowing Your light to shine through my life.

Let my commitment to truth inspire others to seek it as well, creating a community built on honesty and respect.

Thank You for the guidance You provide and for the truth that sets us free.

In your name, I pray,

Amen.

Activity: Script Exploration

Discuss a story from the Bible that highlights the value of honesty (like Ananias and Sapphira).

Day 5: Speaking the Truth in Love

Being honest means that we care about others' feelings. But sometimes, being honest can be hard. There are moments when we might want to hide the truth because we are afraid of hurting someone. But if we come from a place of love, we can find the right words to say. "I really and truly believe you can do better in this game. I'm here to support you!"

When we are honest, we also encourage others to be honest, too. Your honesty could inspire your friends to share their true thoughts. It can create a safe space where everyone feels comfortable to talk. They might say, "I felt left out, too," and now you both can find a way to work on things together. That is how friendships grow stronger.

Journaling

Write about a situation where you had to choose between honesty and kindness.

_____

_____

_____

_____

_____

_____

_____

Scripture

Colossians 3:9: "Do not lie to each other, since you have taken off your old self with its practices" (*Holy Bible NIV: New International Version*, n.d.).

Activity: Drawing

Draw a large heart with hands around it. The hands can represent love and compassion, while the heart symbolizes honesty. Decorate the heart with words or symbols that represent honesty.

Day 6: Forgiveness and Honesty

Scripture

James 5:16: "Therefore confess your sins to each other and pray for each other so that you may be healed" (*Holy Bible NIV: New International Version*, n.d.).

Affirmation

"I know honesty can heal relationships."

Activity: Reflection

Think about someone you need to apologize to and write down how you can be honest with them.

_____

_____

_____

_____

_____

Day 7: End-Of-Week Review

- **Recap:** Discuss and share what you've learned from this week's topic with your family.
- **Scripture:** Proverbs 19:1: "Better the poor whose walk is blameless than a fool whose lips are perverse" (*Holy Bible NIV: New International Version*, n.d.).
- **Family Activity:** End the week by writing a thank-you note to God for the truth and honesty in your life.
- **Preparation for Next Week:** Love is not merely an emotion; it involves actions. It encourages us to perform acts of kindness, forgive freely, and support those in need, embodying the love we receive from God.

Week 14: Love: The Greatest Commandment

Day 1: What Is Love?

Devotion

Love is the greatest commandment and is shown through our actions and words.

Once upon a time, a kind woman named Julia lived in a vibrant village called Bethany. She was known for her warm heart and love for everyone, from the smallest child to the oldest elder. Julia often helped her neighbors and made sure no one felt lonely or sad.

One day, as Julia was preparing a meal for her family, she heard a knock at the door. It was a young boy named Samuel, looking worried. "Julia, my father is sick, and I don't know how to help him," he said with tears in his eyes.

Julia knelt down beside Samuel and said gently, "Don't worry, Samuel. Love is the greatest commandment, and we can show love through our actions." She decided to visit Samuel's father. Together, they brought him soup and flowers to brighten his day.

When they arrived, Samuel's father smiled weakly and said, "Thank you for your kindness. It means so much to me." Seeing the joy in his eyes, Julia and Samuel felt the warmth of love spreading between them.

As they were leaving, Julia reminded Samuel, "Love is not just a feeling; it's something we do. We show love through our words and actions."

One afternoon, Julia noticed a new family in town who looked lost and alone. Remembering how love brings people together, she decided to invite them over for dinner. She cooked a delightful meal and set the table beautifully.

When the new family arrived, they were surprised by the warm welcome. "Thank you for inviting us," the mother said, her eyes glistening with gratitude. Throughout the meal, laughter and stories filled the air, and soon, the new family felt right at home.

As the sun set, Julia looked around at the smiling faces and thought about Rabbi Eli's words. Love truly is the greatest commandment. It brings people together, heals wounds, and creates a sense of belonging.

Scripture

Matthew 22:37-39: "Love the Lord your God with all your heart and with all your soul and with all your mind... Love your neighbor as yourself" (*Holy Bible NIV: New International Version*, n.d.).

Activity: Reflection

Write down what love means to you and how you can show it.

_____

_____

_____

_____

_____

_____

_____

Day 2: God's" Love for Us

Scripture

John 3:16: "For God so loved the world that he gave his one and only Son..." (*Holy Bible NIV: New International Version*, n.d.).

Affirmation

"I am loved by God!"

Activity: Journaling

Write a thank-you note to God for His love and how it makes you feel.

_____

_____

_____

_____

_____

_____

_____

Day 3: Loving Others

Scripture

1 John 4:19: "We love because he first loved us" (*Holy Bible NIV: New International Version*, n.d.).

Discussion

What does it mean to love others the way God loves us, and how can we show that love in our everyday lives?

Activity: Challenge

Perform a random act of kindness for someone today.

Day 4: Love in Action

Scripture

1 Corinthians 13:4-7: "Love is patient, love is kind..." (*Holy Bible NIV: New International Version*, n.d.).

Prayer

Dear God,

Guide me to act selflessly, putting others' needs before my own, and to share Your love in tangible ways.

May I be intentional in my efforts to lift others up, showing them that they are valued and cherished. Thank You for the opportunities You provide for me to share love and kindness.

In your name, I pray,

Amen.

Activity: Art and Craft Project

Create a "Love Tree" where each leaf represents an action of love you can do for someone.

Day 5: Love and Forgiveness

Love helps us to be kind, even when we feel hurt. It's like when your friend accidentally takes your toy without asking. Instead of getting really mad, you can choose to talk about it. You can say, "I didn't like it when you took my toy." This way, you both understand how each other feels.

Love also means sharing what makes us happy. If you have a yummy snack, sharing it with a friend can spread joy. You might say, "Want to share this? It's my favorite!" It makes you both feel good inside. Love is about making each other smile, just like how a hug can make a sad day better.

Journaling

Think about someone you need to forgive, and write down how you can show love to them.

_____

_____

_____

_____

_____

_____

_____

Scripture

Colossians 3:13: "Bear with each other and forgive one another if any of you has a grievance against someone" (*Holy Bible NIV: New International Version*, n.d.).

Activity: Drawing

Design a garden where each flower has a name representing an act of kindness or forgiveness (e.g., "sharing," "apologizing"). Fill the garden with your own ideas of how to spread love and forgiveness.

Day 6: Loving Your Enemies

Scripture

Matthew 5:44: "But I tell you, love your enemies and pray for those who persecute you" (*Holy Bible NIV: New International Version*, n.d.).

Affirmation

"I will show love even to those who hurt me."

Activity: Prayer

Pray for someone who might be a challenge for you to love.

Day 7: End-Of-Week Review

- **Recap:** Discuss and share what you've learned from this week's topic with your family.
- **Scripture:** 1 Thessalonians 5:18: "Give thanks in all circumstances; for this is God's will for you in Christ Jesus" (*Holy Bible NIV: New International Version*, n.d.).
- **Family Activity:** Each family member takes turns sharing what love and forgiveness mean to them. Encourage everyone to speak from the heart and listen without interruption.
- **Preparation for Next Week:** Obeying God's word can be challenging due to personal desires, societal pressures, or misunderstandings. However, overcoming these challenges is part of the journey, and it takes faith and perseverance.

Week 15: Obedience: Following God's Word

Day 1: What Is Obedience?

Devotion

Obedience means listening to God and doing what He says. Just like kids need to listen to their parents, we need to listen to God.

A young boy named Lucas lived in a quaint village between low hills. Lucas loved to play in the fields and explore the nearby woods, but more than anything, he loved his family and listened to their wise words.

One sunny morning, Lucas' father said, "Lucas, remember to obey God's words and do what He asks of you. Just like you listen to me, it's important to listen to God." Lucas nodded, excited to learn more about obedience.

Later that day, Lucas heard a soft whisper while playing near the river. It was a gentle voice calling him, "Lucas, come to the edge of the woods." Curious, Lucas decided to follow the voice, but he remembered his father's words. "Wait," he thought. "I need to be obedient to God and ensure it's safe."

Instead of rushing to the woods, Lucas knelt down and prayed. "Dear God, if this is you asking me to come closer, please show me the way." As he finished praying, he felt a warm breeze and saw a beautiful butterfly flying in a circle above him. He smiled and felt a sense of peace in his heart.

Encouraged by this sign, Lucas proceeded carefully. As he reached the edge of the woods, he noticed a group of children who were lost and looking scared. "What's wrong?" he asked them.

"We were playing hide and seek, and now we can't find our way back home!" one of them said, tears welling in her eyes.

Lucas thought for a moment about how he could help. He remembered what his father taught him about being obedient. "We can all work together! Follow me, and I'll lead you back," he said confidently.

That evening, Lucas shared his adventure with his father. "I prayed and listened, and God showed me the way to help my friends," Lucas explained excitedly. His father hugged him and said, "You see, Lucas? Obedience means listening to God and doing what He says, just like how we listen to our parents. You made a difference today."

Scripture

James 1:22: "Do not merely listen to the word, and so deceive yourselves. Do what it says" (*Holy Bible NIV: New International Version*, n.d.).

Activity: Reflection

Write down one thing you can obey at home.

_____

_____

_____

_____

_____

_____

_____

Day 2: God Can Show You the Way—Trust Him

Reflection

Reflect on a specific command or teaching from God that has positively influenced your actions or decisions.

_____

_____

_____

_____

_____

_____

Scripture

Proverbs 3:5-6: "Trust in the Lord with all your heart and lean not on your own understanding; in all your ways submit to him, and he will make your paths straight" (*Holy Bible NIV: New International Version*, n.d.).

Affirmation

"I trust God to guide my path."

Activity: Drawing

Draw a picture of a flower and write how obeying God helps you grow.

Day 3: Loving and Respecting Your Parents

Scripture

Ephesians 6:1: "Children, obey your parents in the Lord, for this is right" (Holy Bible NIV: New International Version, n.d.).

Discussion

How does listening to our parents and following their guidance show them that we love and respect them?

Activity: Challenge

Write a thank you note to your parents for their love and guidance.

Day 4: Be Brave Like Jesus

Scripture

Luke 22:42: "Father, if you are willing, take this cup from me; yet not my will, but yours be done" (*Holy Bible NIV: New International Version*, n.d.).

Prayer

Dear God,

Just as Jesus showed incredible bravery in living out His purpose, even in the face of adversity, may I draw inspiration from His example.

When I feel afraid or uncertain, remind me that You are always with me, guiding and supporting me. Help me to trust in Your plan for my life, even when the path seems difficult.

May I be bold in serving others and sharing Your message of love and hope. Let my bravery inspire those around me to also act with courage and faith. Thank You for the strength that You provide, and may I always seek to reflect the bravery of Jesus in all that I do.

In Your name, I pray,

Amen.

Activity: Journaling

Journal a time when you chose to obey even when it was difficult.

_____

_____

_____

_____

_____

Day 5: Obeying God Leads to Happiness and Peace

Being patient with our friends and family means waiting for them to understand or finish what they are doing, even if we feel a bit frustrated. When we do this, it shows that we care about them and want to help. Being patient makes our friendships and family bonds stronger, just like how a strong tree needs deep roots to stand tall!

Journaling

How can you show that you are obeying God in your daily life, and what good things have you experienced as a result?

_____

_____

_____

_____

_____

_____

_____

Scripture

Deuteronomy 28:1-2: "If you fully obey the Lord your God and carefully follow all his commands I give you today, the Lord your God will set you high above all the nations on earth. All these blessings will come on you and accompany you if you obey the Lord your God" (*Holy Bible NIV: New International Version*, n.d.).

Activity: Drawing

Draw a scene where you are obeying God. This could be helping someone, being kind to a friend, or doing your chores without being asked.

Sharing Opportunity

Share your drawing with your family.

Day 6: Learning From Our Mistakes

Scripture

Jonah 1:1-3: "The word of the Lord came to Jonah, son of Amittai: 'Go to the great city of Nineveh and preach against it because its wickedness has come up before me.' But Jonah ran away from the Lord and headed for Tarshish. He went down to Joppa, where he found a ship bound for that port. After paying the fare, he went aboard and sailed for Tarshish to flee from the Lord" (*Holy Bible NIV: New International Version*, n.d.).

Affirmation

"I learn from my mistakes and try again."

Activity: Challenge

Act out the story of Jonah with a friend or family member.

Day 7: End-Of-Week Review

- **Recap:** Discuss and share what you've learned from this week's topic with your family.
- **Scripture:** Psalm 119:32: "I run in the path of your commands, for you have broadened my understanding" (*Holy Bible NIV: New International Version*, n.d.).
- **Family Activity:**
  - Create a list of simple commands or actions that reflect God's teachings (e.g., "Help a friend," "Share something," "Say a kind word").
  - Write each command on a slip of paper and put them in a bowl.
  - Gather in a circle.
  - Take turns drawing a slip of paper from the bowl.
  - Read the command aloud and then act it out or talk about a time you followed that command.
- **Preparation for Next Week:** When we view ourselves through the lens of faith, we acknowledge that our abilities and achievements are gifts from God, cultivating an attitude of gratitude rather than pride. Humility allows us to treat others with kindness and respect, appreciating their worth as individuals created in God's image.

Week 16: Humility: Being Modest and Respectful

Day 1: What Is Humility?

Devotion

Being humble means thinking of others first and not bragging. It's important to lift others up!

A kind man named Jonah lived in a bustling town by the sea. He was known for his gentle spirit and humble heart. Jonah worked as a fisherman, bringing home fish to feed his family and share with those in need.

One afternoon, as Jonah was returning to the market with his catch, he noticed a group of fishermen gathered around a man named Simon. Simon was boasting loudly about how many fish he had caught that day. "Look at my huge load! I'm the best fisherman in the whole town!" he bragged, puffing out his chest with pride.

Jonah felt a little sad hearing Simon's words. Instead of feeling joy for his neighbor's success, Simon's bragging seemed to push others down. Jonah believed that true greatness comes from lifting others, not from boasting about oneself.

Inspired by this thought, Jonah decided to take action. He approached Simon with a warm smile and said, "Simon, your skills are remarkable! I saw the size of your fish today; they're truly impressive! Would you like to share your fishing techniques with some of the younger fishermen? They would be grateful to learn from you."

Simon, taken aback by Jonah's kindness, hesitated for a moment. "Well, I suppose I could," he replied, looking a little confused. But Jonah wasn't finished. He continued, "It's a wonderful opportunity for all of us to grow together. When we help each other, our community becomes stronger."

Soon, Jonah gathered the other fishermen, and with Simon leading, they spent the afternoon learning new techniques and sharing stories. The joy of teamwork filled the air, and everyone felt included. As they helped one another, Simon realized how much brighter the day was when they worked together instead of boasting alone.

From that day on, Simon learned a valuable lesson about humility and kindness. He saw how Jonah's selflessness transformed the fishing community into a close-knit family where everyone rejoiced in each other's accomplishments.

Scripture

Philippians 2:3: "Do nothing out of selfish ambition or vain conceit. Rather, in humility, value others above yourselves" (*Holy Bible NIV: New International Version*, n.d.).

Activity: Reflection

Write down ways to show humility.

_____

_____

_____

_____

_____

_____

_____

Day 2: Serve Others as Jesus Did

Reflection

How does Jesus' example of servanthood challenge you to reconsider your own approach to serving others in your daily life?

Activity: Reflection

Write down ways to show humility.

_____

_____

_____

_____

_____

_____

_____

Scripture

Mark 10:45: "For even the Son of Man did not come to be served, but to serve, and to give his life as a ransom for many" (*Holy Bible NIV: New International Version*, n.d.).

Affirmation

"I find joy in serving others."

Activity: Drawing

Draw a picture of you helping someone.

Day 3: Being a Good Friend

Scripture

Romans 12:10: "Be devoted to one another in love. Honor one another above yourselves" (*Holy Bible NIV: New International Version*, n.d.).

Discussion

Why is it important to treat our friends with respect and support them, just like we would want to be treated?

Activity: Challenge

Write a letter of appreciation to a friend.

Day 4: Being a Good Listener

Scripture

James 1:19: "My dear brothers and sisters, take note of this: Everyone should be quick to listen, slow to speak, and slow to become angry" (*Holy Bible NIV: New International Version*, n.d.).

Prayer

Dear God,

Help me to be a good listener. Grant me the patience to hear the words of others with an open heart and mind. May I be quick to understand, slow to respond, and even slower to judge.

Teach me to cherish the thoughts and feelings of those around me. Guide me to communicate with love and empathy, reflecting Your grace in every interaction.

Amen.

Activity: Meditation

Sit quietly for a few minutes and think about how you can listen better.

Day 5: We Should Thank God for Our Blessings

Gratitude means being thankful for the good things we have in our lives. When we feel grateful, we realize how lucky we are, and it helps us be humble, which means not thinking we are better than others. Saying thank you to God for our blessings, like our family, friends, and nice experiences, helps us remember to appreciate what we have. It's like looking at a beautiful picture and feeling happy about it. Being grateful makes our hearts feel warm and encourages us to share kindness with others because we understand how important these blessings are in our lives!

Journaling

Write about at least three blessings you're grateful for.

1. _____

2. _____

3. _____

Scripture

1 Thessalonians 5:18: "Give thanks in all circumstances; for this is God's will for you in Christ Jesus" (*Holy Bible NIV: New International Version*, n.d.).

Activity: Drawing

Draw leaves, and on each leaf, write one way you can show humility or gratitude in your daily life, such as helping others or saying thank you.

Day 6: Helping Others Is an Act of Love

Scripture

Luke 10:30-37: "In reply, Jesus said: 'A man was going down from Jerusalem to Jericho, when he was attacked by robbers. They stripped him of his clothes, beat him, and went away, leaving him half dead. A priest happened to be going down the same road, and when he saw the man, he passed by on the other side. So, too, a Levite, when he came to the place and saw him, passed by on the other side. But a Samaritan, as he traveled, came where the man was, and when he saw him, he took pity on him. He went to him and bandaged his wounds, pouring on oil and wine. Then he put the man on his own donkey, brought him to an inn, and took care of him. The next day, he took out two denarii and gave them to the innkeeper. 'Look after him,' he said, 'and when I return, I will reimburse you for any extra expense you may have.' Which of these three do you think was a neighbor to the man who fell into the hands of robbers? The expert in the law replied, 'The one who had mercy on him.' Jesus told him, 'Go and do likewise'" (*Holy Bible NIV: New International Version*, n.d.).

Affirmation

"I can help those in need."

Activity: Service Project

Help out a neighbor with chores.

Day 7: End-Of-Week Review

- **Recap:** Discuss and share what you've learned from this week's topic with your family.
- **Scripture:** Proverbs 11:2: "When pride comes, then comes disgrace, but with humility comes wisdom" (*Holy Bible NIV: New International Version*, n.d.).
- **Family Activity:** Over a week, each family member writes down one act of humility they practiced or witnessed each day. This could be helping someone, saying thank you, or admitting when they were wrong. At the end of the week, gather as a family to share what everyone wrote. Take turns reading the slips of paper aloud, discussing the impact of these humble actions on themselves and others.
- **Preparation for Next Week:** When we give generously, we not only fulfill the needs of others but also foster a sense of community and connection, reinforcing the values of kindness and compassion. Generosity enriches our own lives, bringing joy and fulfillment, as it reflects the love and grace we have received and allows us to participate in making the world a better place.

Week 17: Generosity: Giving From the Heart

Day 1: What Is Generosity?

Devotion

Generosity is about giving from our hearts, whether it's our time, money, or love.

A cheerful girl named Ruth lived in a lively village surrounded by beautiful hills. Ruth had a heart full of love and kindness. She loved to help others, whether it was sharing her toys with her friends or helping her mother bake cookies for the neighbors.

One bright morning, Ruth heard a knock on her door. It was her friend, Abigail, looking worried. "Ruth, my family is having a hard time. My father's job has been slow, and we're not sure how we'll have enough food for dinner," Abigail said, her eyes downcast.

Ruth's heart sank for her friend. She remembered the delicious cookies her mother had baked the day before. She thought about how their family always shared their blessings with others. "Don't worry, Abigail! Let's go to my house and share some of the cookies with your family. We can help!"

As they arrived at Ruth's house, she quickly filled a basket with cookies and added some fruits from the kitchen. "This is a small way we can help," Ruth smiled. "Sometimes, a little generosity makes a big difference!"

Abigail's eyes lit up with joy. "Thank you, Ruth! Your kindness means so much!"

After delivering the basket, Ruth felt a warm glow inside. She loved giving from her heart, and she knew that generosity brings happiness not only to those who receive but also to those who give.

From that day on, Ruth continued to look for ways to share her love and help her community. The spirit of generosity grew in the village, inspiring many to give from their hearts and create a caring and united community. And Ruth knew that true happiness comes from giving, just as much as it does from receiving.

Scripture

2 Corinthians 9:7: "Each of you should give what you have decided in your heart to give, not reluctantly or under compulsion, for God loves a cheerful giver" (*Holy Bible NIV: New International Version*, n.d.).

Activity: Reflection

Think of ways you can give to others.

___
___
___
___
___
___
___

Day 2: True Abundance

Reflection

Reflect on a time when you had to give or serve from a place of scarcity rather than abundance.

___
___
___
___
___
___
___

Scripture

Mark 12:41-44: "Jesus sat down opposite the place where the offerings were put and watched the crowd putting their money into the temple treasury. Many rich people threw in large amounts. But a poor widow came and put in two very small copper coins worth only a few cents. Calling his disciples to him, Jesus said, 'Truly I tell you, this poor widow has put more into the treasury than all the others. They all gave out of their wealth, but she, out of her poverty, put in everything—all she had to live on.'" (*Holy Bible NIV: New International Version*, n.d.).

Affirmation

"Every gift counts, no matter how small."

Activity: Drawing

Draw a picture of something you want to share with someone.

Day 3: Showing True Generosity

Scripture

Proverbs 19:17: "Whoever is generous to the poor lends to the Lord, and he will repay him for his deed" (*Holy Bible NIV: New International Version*, n.d.).

Discussion

What are some ways we can help others who are in need, and how does that show true generosity in our hearts?

Activity: Challenge

Collect gently used clothes and donate them to a local shelter or thrift shop.

Day 4: Sharing Is Caring

Scripture

Acts 20:35: "In everything I did, I showed you that by this kind of hard work, we must help the weak, remembering the words the Lord Jesus himself said: 'It is more blessed to give than to receive'" (*Holy Bible NIV: New International Version*, n.d.).

Prayer

Dear God,

Help me to share freely. Instill in my heart a spirit of generosity, encouraging me to give without hesitation or expectation.

May I embrace opportunities to uplift others through my kindness and support. Let my willingness to share reflect Your love and grace in the world.

Amen.

Activity

Journal about a time when sharing made you happy.

_____

_____

_____

_____

_____

_____

_____

Day 5: Giving Time to Help Others

Helping others isn't just about giving them toys or food; it's also important to share our time. When we spend time helping someone, like playing with a friend who feels lonely or helping a parent with chores, we show we care. Giving our time can make others feel happy and supported, just like getting a present. It's a special gift that we can all give. When we help others with our time, we make the world a better place and build strong friendships. Remember, the love and kindness we share make a big difference, just like the things we give!

Journaling

How can you find ways in your daily life to give your time to help others, and what impact do you think your actions could have on those around you?

_____

_____

_____

_____

_____

_____

_____

Scripture

Galatians 6:9: "Let us not become weary in doing good, for at the proper time we will reap a harvest if we do not give up" (*Holy Bible NIV: New International Version*, n.d.).

Activity: Drawing

Draw a scene that represents the importance of giving time to help others. For example, helping a neighbor with yard work, reading a book to younger children, volunteering at a local shelter or food bank, or playing with friends who may feel lonely.

Day 6: Encouraging Others With Kind Words

Scripture

Proverbs 16:24: "Gracious words are a honeycomb, sweet to the soul and healing to the bones" (*Holy Bible NIV: New International Version*, n.d.).

Affirmation

"I choose to speak kindly."

Activity: Challenge

Write kind notes for friends or family.

Day 7: End-Of-Week Review

- **Recap:** Discuss and share what you've learned from this week's topic with your family.
- **Scripture:** Luke 6:38: "Give, and it will be given to you; a good measure, pressed down, shaken together and running over, will be poured into your lap. For with the measure you use, it will be measured to you" (*Holy Bible NIV: New International Version*, n.d.).

- **Family Activity:** Create a Pictionary-style game where you draw faith-related words or phrases (like "sharing," "community," or "kindness") and teammates must guess what they are.
- **Preparation for Next Week:** When we are faithful, we demonstrate our dedication to following through on our word, even in challenging circumstances, which fosters strong bonds and encourages mutual respect.

Week 18: Faithfulness: Keeping Your Promises

Day 1: Celebrate God's Faithfulness

Devotion

Being faithful means keeping our promises and being trustworthy. Just like we can rely on God, people should rely on us, too.

In a sunny little town called Hebron, there lived a young boy named Daniel. Daniel was known for his bright smile and friendly nature. He loved playing with his friends and helping his family. But more than anything, Daniel valued keeping promises and being someone others could trust.

One day, Daniel's father said to him, "Daniel, I need you to help me with an important task this weekend. We have a lot of work to do in the garden, and I need you to promise me you'll be there to help." Daniel replied with great enthusiasm, "I promise, Dad! I will be there to help you."

As the week went by, Daniel's friend Caleb invited him to a fun picnic by the river on the same day he had promised to help his father. At first, Daniel was torn. "The picnic will be so much fun! But I promised my dad," he thought. Remembering how much he loved spending time with his father, Daniel made a decision.

When the day of the picnic arrived, Daniel chose to honor his promise. He worked side by side with his father, planting seeds and watering the flowers. They laughed and shared stories while they worked, making the garden look beautiful. Daniel's father noticed his hard work and said, "I'm so proud of you, Daniel. You kept your promise, and that shows how faithful you are."

Later that day, as they were finishing up, Daniel felt happy inside. He realized that being faithful means keeping our promises and being someone that others can rely on.

From that day on, Daniel continued to keep his promises, and his friends began to notice. They often came to him for help, knowing he would always be there for them, just like he was for his father.

Scripture

Lamentations 3:22-23: "Because of the Lord's great love we are not consumed, for his compassions never fail. They are new every morning; great is your faithfulness" (*Holy Bible NIV: New International Version*, n.d.).

Activity: Reflection

Write down promises you want to keep.

___

Day 2: Being Grateful for God's Faithfulness

Reflection

Reflect on a time when you experienced God's faithfulness in your life. How can you hold onto that experience to strengthen your trust in Him during difficult times?

Scripture

Deuteronomy 7:9: "Know therefore that the Lord your God is God; he is the faithful God, keeping his covenant of love to a thousand generations of those who love him and keep his commandments" (*Holy Bible NIV: New International Version*, n.d.).

Affirmation

"God is faithful and true."

Activity: Drawing

Draw something that reminds you of God's faithfulness.

Day 3: Keeping Promises

Scripture

Matthew 5:37: "Let what you say be simply 'Yes' or 'No'; anything more than this comes from evil" (*Holy Bible NIV: New International Version*, n.d.).

Discussion

Why do you think keeping promises to our friends is a sign that we care about them, and how does it make our friendships stronger?

Activity: Journaling

Journal about a time you kept a promise to a friend.

_____

_____

_____

_____

_____

_____

_____

Day 4: Doing My Best in Everything I Do

Scripture

Colossians 3:23: "Whatever you do, work at it with all your heart, as working for the Lord, not for human masters" (*Holy Bible NIV: New International Version*, n.d.).

Prayer

Dear God,

Help me to work hard in all that I do. Encourage me to give my best effort in every task. May I approach my work with passion and dedication, seeing it as an opportunity to serve You.

Guide my actions and decisions to reflect Your love and purpose in my life.

Amen.

Activity: Challenge

Create a checklist of daily chores or tasks to complete.

Day 5: Being Faithful in Our Prayers

Being faithful in our prayers means talking to God often, like having a good friend to chat with. When we pray, we share our thoughts, feelings, and wishes, just like telling someone about our day. Trusting God and believing that He listens to us and cares about what we say is important. Even when things are tough, we can feel safe knowing God is there for us. Remember, just like watering a plant helps it grow, praying helps our faith grow stronger every day!

Journaling

How has being faithful in your prayers impacted your relationship with God, and what challenges do you face in maintaining that consistency?

_____

_____

_____

_____

_____

_____

_____

Scripture

1 Thessalonians 5:17: "Pray continually" (*Holy Bible NIV: New International Version*, n.d.).

Activity: Drawing

Draw a picture representing how we can listen for God's guidance (like an ear, a heart, or a peaceful scene).

Day 6: Following God Faithfully

Scripture

Genesis 6:22: "Noah did everything just as God commanded him" (*Holy Bible NIV: New International Version*, n.d.).

Affirmation

"I will follow God's plan for my life."

Activity: Challenge

Read the story of Noah (Genesis 6:9 to Genesis 9:17) and act out a scene from it.

Day 7: End-Of-Week Review

- **Recap:** Discuss and share what you've learned from this week's topic with your family.
- **Scripture**: Proverbs 28:20: "A faithful person will be richly blessed, but one eager to get rich will not go unpunished" (*Holy Bible NIV: New International Version*, n.d.).
- **Family Activity**: Create bingo cards with different acts of faith, kindness, or sharing activities (like "help a friend," "volunteer," or "share a toy"). When you complete an activity, they can mark it off. The first to get a bingo shares their experiences with the group.
- **Preparation for Next Week:** Self-control is the essential ability to make the right choices, even in the face of temptation and distraction. It is a fruit of the Spirit, reflecting a person's commitment to live according to God's will rather than being swayed by immediate desires or impulses.

Week 19: Self-Control: Making Right Choices

Day 1: What Is Self-Control?

Devotion

Self-control is about making good choices, even when it's hard. It's like training our hearts and minds.

In the ancient land of Israel, there was a young girl named Emma. She was known for her cheerful spirit and her love for adventure.

One day, while exploring the fields near her home, Emma discovered a beautiful garden filled with the most colorful flowers she had ever seen. It belonged to a man named Eli, who was known for his lovely garden and delicious fruits.

Eli was a kind but busy man, often working in his garden to keep it healthy and flourishing. As Emma looked at the fruits, "I want to pick just one fruit to taste," she whispered to herself. But then she remembered her mother's words: "Emma, always show respect for others' belongings. Make good choices, even when it's hard."

Emma paused, struggling with her thoughts. "It would be easy to take one fruit, and Eli won't notice, but it wouldn't be right," she thought. She knew that self-control meant making good choices, even if it was tempting to give in to her desires.

Just then, she spotted Eli coming toward the garden. As he approached, Emma felt nervous. She decided to greet him instead. "Hello, Mr. Eli! Your garden looks beautiful today!" she called out with a smile.

Eli stopped and smiled back. "Thank you, Emma! It takes hard work to keep it that way. Would you like to help me?"

Emma's heart filled with joy. "I would love to help!" After spending the afternoon tending to the flowers and enjoying their scents, Emma felt grateful for Eli's kindness. Just before she left, Eli picked two ripe fruits from a nearby tree and handed them to her. "Here, Emma! I want you to have these as a thank-you for your help."

Emma's eyes widened in surprise. "Thank you so much, Mr. Eli! This is very generous of you!" she exclaimed, realizing that she didn't need to take what wasn't hers when she could receive gifts out of kindness.

As Emma walked home, she felt proud of her choice to respect Eli's garden. She knew that practicing self-control was like training her heart and mind to make the right decisions. That moment taught her an important lesson about patience, respect, and kindness.

Activity: Reflection

Write down a time you made a good choice.

_____

_____

_____

_____

_____

_____

_____

Scripture

Galatians 5:22-23: "But the fruit of the Spirit is love, joy, peace, forbearance, kindness, goodness, faithfulness, gentleness and self-control. Against such things, there is no law" (*Holy Bible NIV: New International Version*, n.d.).

Day 2: Making Good Decisions

Reflection

How can using self-control in everyday situations can make me happier and more peaceful?

_____

_____

_____

_____

_____

_____

_____

Scripture

Proverbs 25:28: "Like a city whose walls are broken through is a person who lacks self-control" (*Holy Bible NIV: New International Version*, n.d.).

Affirmation

"I am strong in my decisions."

Activity: Drawing

Draw a picture showing a good choice vs. a bad choice.

Day 3: Conquering Temptation With Jesus

Scripture

Matthew 4:1-11: "Then Jesus was led by the Spirit into the wilderness to be tempted by the devil. After fasting forty days and forty nights, he was hungry. The tempter came to him and said, 'If you are the Son of God, tell these stones to become bread.' Jesus answered, 'It is written: Man shall not live on bread alone, but on every word that comes from the mouth of God.

"Then, the devil took him to the holy city and had him stand on the highest point of the temple. 'If you are the Son of God,' he said, 'throw yourself down. For it is written: He will command his angels concerning you, and they will lift you up in their hands, so that you will not strike your foot against a stone.

"Jesus answered him, 'It is also written: Do not put the Lord your God to the test.'

"Again, the devil took him to a very high mountain and showed him all the kingdoms of the world and their splendor. 'All this I will give you,' he said, 'if you will bow down and worship me.'

"Jesus said to him, 'Away from me, Satan! For it is written: Worship the Lord your God, and serve him only.'

Then the devil left him, and angels came and attended him" (*Holy Bible NIV: New International Version*, n.d.).

Discussion

How can we use Jesus' example of self-control to help us make good choices when we're faced with temptations?

Activity: Journaling

Journal about a time you faced a temptation and how you handled it.

_____

_____

_____

_____

_____

_____

_____

Day 4: Thinking Before Speaking

Scripture

Proverbs 13:3: "Those who guard their lips preserve their lives, but those who speak rashly will come to ruin" (*Holy Bible NIV: New International Version*, n.d.).

Prayer

Dear God,

Help me use my words to bless others. Empower me to speak with kindness, encouragement, and truth.

May my words uplift those around me and inspire hope and love. Let my voice be a source of healing and joy in the lives of others.

Amen.

Activity: Challenge

Create a list of kind words to use daily.

Day 5: Remaining Calm and Patient

Self-control means being able to manage our feelings and reactions, especially when we feel strong emotions like anger. When something happens that makes us upset, instead of shouting or getting mad right away, we can take a deep breath and think about how we want to respond. It's like being a superhero for our feelings; we can choose how to act instead of letting our emotions take charge. For instance, if a friend takes our toy, instead of getting angry, we can calmly talk to them about sharing. Learning self-control helps us make better choices and keeps us and others around us happy.

Reflection

How can you practice controlling your feelings, like anger, in a positive way when you feel upset?

_____

_____

_____

_____

_____

Scripture

James 1:19-20: "My dear brothers and sisters, take note of this: Everyone should be quick to listen, slow to speak and slow to become angry because human anger does not produce the righteousness that God desires" (*Holy Bible NIV: New International Version*, n.d.).

Activity: Drawing

1. Start with a large circle on a piece of paper. Divide the circle into sections like a pie chart, with each section representing different feelings (e.g., anger, happiness, sadness, disappointment, etc.).
2. Label each section with a feeling and include a few words or drawings that represent how that feeling might look (e.g., for anger, a red face with clenched fists).
3. In each section, draw or write one way to control that feeling positively. For example, for anger, they might draw someone taking deep breaths, counting to ten, or talking it out with a friend.

Day 6: Pleasing God Through Self-Control

Scripture

1 Corinthians 10:31: "So whether you eat or drink or whatever you do, do it all for the glory of God" (*Holy Bible NIV: New International Version*, n.d.).

Affirmation

"I choose to honor God in everything I do."

Activity: Challenge

Create a large decision tree on a poster board with various life choices (e.g., dealing with peer pressure, handling arguments). Explore the possible consequences of each choice and write your reflections on sticky notes.

Day 7: End-Of-Week Review

- **Recap:** Discuss and share what you've learned from this week's topic with your family.
- **Scripture:** 2 Timothy 1:72: "For the Spirit God gave us does not make us timid, but gives us power, love and self-discipline" (*Holy Bible NIV: New International Version*, n.d.).
- **Family Activity:** Create a self-control challenge to follow for the week.
- **Preparation for Next Week:** By embracing a heart of thankfulness, we can cultivate joy in our daily lives, regardless of our situations.

Week 20: Contentment: Being Happy With What You Have

Day 1: What Is Contentment?

Devotion

Contentment means being happy with what we have instead of wanting more.

Once, in a peaceful land, there lived a man named Job. Job was known far and wide for his kindness and generosity. He had a wonderful family, a beautiful home, and many animals that helped him in his daily life. Job was content with what he had, and he thanked God for his blessings every day.

One day, a great storm struck Job's land. Winds howled, and rain poured down. When the storm finally passed, Job's fields were in ruins, and he had lost many of his animals. His heart felt heavy, but Job didn't lose hope. He knelt down and prayed, thanking God for the blessings he still had, like his loving family and the health he enjoyed.

As time went on, more misfortunes came Job's way. He faced challenges and hardships that made him question everything. His friends came to comfort him, and they encouraged him to complain and despair. But Job, even in his sadness, chose to remain thankful for what he still had. He remembered the beauty of the sunset, the laughter of his children, and the love around him.

One day, Job's friends asked him, "How can you still be happy when you've lost so much?" Job replied, "Even when things are tough, I have learned to be content. Happiness comes not from what we own, but from appreciating the love and joy in our lives."

Through his trials, Job discovered that true contentment is about being grateful for what we have, no matter how little it may seem.

Scripture

Philippians 4:11-12: "I am not saying this because I am in need, for I have learned to be content whatever the circumstances. I know what it is to be in need, and I know what it is to have plenty. I have learned the secret of being content in any and every situation, whether well fed or hungry, whether living in plenty or in want" (*Holy Bible NIV: New International Version*, n.d.).

Activity: Reflection

Reflect on a situation where you felt discontent. What were the underlying reasons, and how could you have reframed your thinking to find happiness in what you had instead?

_____

_____

_____

_____

_____

_____

_____

Day 2: Cherish Your Blessings

Reflection

How can I celebrate and embrace my unique qualities rather than measuring my worth against others?

_____

_____

_____

_____

_____

_____

_____

Scripture

2 Corinthians 10:12: "We do not dare to classify or compare ourselves with some who commend themselves. When they measure themselves by themselves and compare themselves with themselves, they are not wise" (*Holy Bible NIV: New International Version.*, n.d.).

Affirmation

"I focus on my own blessings."

Activity: Drawing

Draw a picture of what makes you special.

Day 3: Showing Love and Appreciation to Your Friends and Family

Scripture

Proverbs 15:17: "Better a small serving of vegetables with love than a fattened calf with hatred" (*Holy Bible NIV: New International Version*, n.d.).

Discussion

How does being content and appreciating our friends and family help us recognize them as the special gifts they are in our lives?

Activity: Journaling

Journal about your favorite memories with friends.

_____

_____

_____

_____

_____

_____

_____

Day 4: Appreciating God's Creation

Scripture

Psalm 104:24-25: "How many are your works, Lord! In wisdom, you made them all; the earth is full of your creatures. There is the sea, vast and spacious, teeming with creatures beyond number—living things both large and small" (*Holy Bible NIV: New International Version*, n.d.).

Prayer

Dear God,

Thank You for the wonders of nature. Help me to appreciate the mountains, rivers, plants, and all living creatures as reflections of Your glory.

May I find joy and peace in the natural world, and inspire me to care for it with love and respect.

In Your Holy Name,

Amen.

Activity: Challenge

Go outside, observe, and draw something beautiful in nature.

Day 5: Finding Joy in Sharing

Sharing our blessings means giving some of the good things we have to others. When we share, like toys, snacks, or even our time, it makes us feel happy and content inside. When we see others enjoying what we've shared, we feel warm and fuzzy in our hearts. Sharing teaches us kindness and shows that we care. It's also fun to be part of someone else's happiness! And the more we give, the more joy we can create together.

Reflection

How can you share your blessings with others to make both you and them feel happy and content?

_____

_____

_____

_____

_____

_____

_____

Scripture

Acts 20:35: "In all things I have shown you that by working hard in this way, we must help the weak and remember the words of the Lord Jesus, how he himself said, 'It is more blessed to give than to receive'" (*Holy Bible NIV: New International Version*, n.d.).

Activity: Drawing

Draw a scene in a park where children are playing together, sharing toys and snacks. One child can be sharing a ball with others, while another is handing out cookies. Add happy expressions on their faces, and include a sun shining brightly in the sky to represent joy. Behind them, draw a tree with a sign that says "Sharing is Caring!" to emphasize the theme.

Day 6: Thank You, God

Scripture

Colossians 3:15: "And let the peace of Christ rule in your hearts, to which indeed you were called in one body. And be thankful" (*Holy Bible NIV: New International Version*, n.d.).

Affirmation

"I express thankfulness daily."

Activity: Challenge

Write a gratitude letter to God.

Day 7: End-Of-Week Review

- **Recap:** Discuss and share what you've learned from this week's topic with your family.
- **Scripture:** 1 Timothy 6:6-7: "But godliness with contentment is great gain. For we brought nothing into the world, and we cannot take anything out of the world" (*Holy Bible NIV: New International Version*, n.d.).
- **Family Activity:** Play a fun game that centers around sharing and gratitude.

- **Preparation for Next Week:** True friends lift each other up, offering encouragement and understanding in times of need. They share laughter, create lasting memories, and navigate life's challenges together, reminding us that we are never alone.

Week 21: Friendship: Loving and Supporting Each Other

Day 1: The Power of Friendship

Devotion

Friends are there for us through good times and bad. A true friend listens and shows kindness.

In the ancient city of Bethlehem, there lived two close friends named David and Jonathan. David was a young shepherd who had recently been anointed by the prophet Samuel to be the future king of Israel. Jonathan was the son of King Saul, the reigning king, and he was known for his bravery and wisdom. Despite their different backgrounds, the two boys forged a deep and unbreakable bond.

One afternoon, while tending the sheep in the fields, David shared his fears with Jonathan. "I feel so overwhelmed by the weight of becoming king. What if I fail? What if the people don't accept me?" he confessed, his voice filled with uncertainty.

Jonathan listened intently, nodding in understanding. "David, you are brave and chosen by God. Remember, true strength comes from trusting in Him. I believe in you!" he said, placing a reassuring hand on David's shoulder.

One night, Jonathan decided to warn David. He cautiously approached David while the stars twinkled above them. "David, my father is planning to kill you! You must flee to the wilderness to protect yourself," Jonathan urged, his heart heavy with sorrow.

David felt a wave of gratitude. "How will I ever thank you for your kindness, Jonathan?" he asked, realizing the danger Jonathan was in just by helping him.

"Your safety is all that matters to me. As long as you live, our friendship will remain strong," Jonathan replied, determined.

Before parting ways, they made a pact with each other. "No matter what happens, we will always look out for each other and our families," Jonathan vowed.

Through David and Jonathan's story, we see that true friendship endures through trials, sacrifices, and unwavering support. The power of friendship can provide strength, encouragement, and love that lasts beyond even the most difficult of circumstances.

Scripture

Proverbs 17:17: "A friend loves at all times" (*Holy Bible NIV: New International Version*, n.d.).

Activity: Challenge

How can you extend the kindness you've received to others in your life? Think about opportunities to be a true friend to someone who may be in need of a listening ear or a kind gesture.

_____

_____

_____

_____

_____

_____

_____

Day 2: Support Your Friends

Reflection

How can I draw inspiration from Jesus' example of compassion to improve my ability to comfort others in their moments of sadness?

_____

_____

_____

_____

_____

_____

Scripture

Ecclesiastes 4:9-10: "Two are better than one" (*Holy Bible NIV: New International Version*, n.d.).

Affirmation

"I support and encourage my friends."

Activity: Challenge

Create a card for a friend who may be going through a tough time.

Day 3: Share Joy With Friends

Scripture

Proverbs 27:17: "As iron sharpens iron, so one person sharpens another" (*Holy Bible NIV: New International Version*, n.d.).

Discussion

How do we create happy memories with our friends during celebrations, and why is laughing and enjoying time together important for our friendships?

Activity: Challenge

Plan a fun game or activity to do with friends.

Day 4: Forgiving Each Other

Scripture

Colossians 3:13: "Forgive as the Lord forgave you" (*Holy Bible NIV: New International Version*, n.d.).

Prayer

Dear God,

Help me to forgive my friends just like You forgive me. Grant me the strength to let go of any hurt and resentment I may hold. Thank You for Your endless mercy and for guiding me to be a better friend.

Amen.

Activity: Journaling

Write about a time you were forgiven or had to forgive a friend.

_____

_____

_____

_____

_____

_____

_____

Day 5: Being a Good Listener

Listening to each other is really important in friendship because it shows we care about what our friends have to say. When we listen without interrupting, we give our friends a chance to share their thoughts and feelings. It's like giving them a special gift! Good friends pay attention and show that they value each other's words. Additionally, when we listen well, it helps us understand them better and makes our friendship stronger. If a friend is happy or sad, just being there to listen can make a big difference.

Journaling

How does it make you feel when a friend truly listens to you, and what are some ways you can show that you are listening to them?

___

___

___

___

___

___

___

___

Scripture

James 1:19: "Be quick to listen, slow to speak" (*Holy Bible NIV: New International Version*, n.d.).

Activity: Drawing

Create a drawing of two friends sitting together on a park bench. One friend is sharing their feelings, with a speech bubble showing little hearts and stars to represent their emotions. The other friend is leaning in with an attentive expression, holding a notepad and pencil as if they're taking notes. Surround them with colorful flowers and butterflies to symbolize a safe and caring environment for sharing feelings.

Day 6: Encouraging Each Other

Scripture

Hebrews 10:24-25: "Let us consider how we may spur one another on toward love and good deeds" (*Holy Bible NIV: New International Version*, n.d.).

Affirmation

"I cheer my friends on!"

Activity: Challenge

Choose a friend and give them a compliment or encourage them in something they are working on.

Day 7: End-Of-Week Review

- **Recap:** Discuss and share what you've learned from this week's topic with your family.
- **Scripture:** 1 John 4:7: "Dear friends, let us love one another" (*Holy Bible NIV: New International Version*, n.d.).

- **Family and Friends Activity:** Create a "Friendship Chain" by writing kind notes to friends and linking them together.
- **Preparation for Next Week:** Worship is not limited to singing songs or attending church; it encompasses honoring God in every aspect of our lives. It invites us to recognize His presence in our daily routines, relationships, and decisions, reflecting our love and reverence for Him.

Week 22: Worship: Honoring God in Everything

Day 1: How to Worship God

Devotion

Worship is showing love and respect to God. We can worship in many ways, like singing, praying, and being thankful.

In ancient Israel, there was a faithful man named Daniel. He lived in the city of Babylon, far from his homeland. Despite the challenges he faced in a foreign land, Daniel remained devoted to God. Each day, he would set aside time to pray and worship, honoring the God he loved with all his heart.

One day, King Darius issued a decree that for 30 days, no one could pray to any god or human except him. The king wanted to be honored and respected as the ultimate authority. Many in the kingdom praised the king, but Daniel knew that he could not stop worshiping the one true God.

When Daniel learned about the decree, he returned home and went to his upstairs room. He opened the big window facing Jerusalem and knelt down to pray, just as he had always done. With a heart full of love and respect for God, he prayed and gave thanks, knowing that his worship was a beautiful expression of his faith.

Though he knew the risks he faced, Daniel chose to honor God above all else. His dedication and commitment to worship did not go unnoticed. Some of the king's officials, envious of Daniel's favor with the king, caught him praying and rushed to inform King Darius.

Bound by his own decree, the king was distressed upon hearing that Daniel had defied it. "May your God, whom you serve continually, rescue you," Darius said, but he had no choice but to order Daniel to be thrown into the lions' den as punishment.

That night, King Darius could not sleep, anxiously waiting for the dawn. As morning light broke, he hurried to the lions' den. With a trembling voice, he called out, "Daniel, servant of the living God! Has your God, whom you serve continually, been able to rescue you from the lions?"

To the king's astonishment, Daniel answered, "O king, live forever! My God sent His angel, and He shut the mouths of the lions. They have not hurt me because I was found innocent in His sight. I have done no wrong before you, O king."

Overjoyed, King Darius commanded that Daniel be lifted from the den. He then issued a new decree stating that everyone in his kingdom must fear and revere the God of Daniel. The king proclaimed, "For He is the living God and endures forever; His kingdom will not be destroyed, and His dominion will never end."

Scripture

Psalm 95:6: "Come, let us bow down in worship" (*Holy Bible NIV: New International Version*, n.d.).

Activity: Reflection

What does worship mean to you personally, and how do you express your love for God in your daily life?

_____

_____

_____

_____

_____

_____

_____

Day 2: God Loves When We Worship Him Joyfully!

Reflection

How can I incorporate more joy and enthusiasm into my worship practices to reflect my love and gratitude toward God?

_____

_____

_____

_____

_____

_____

_____

Scripture

Psalm 100:1-2: "Shout for joy to the Lord!" (*Holy Bible NIV: New International Version*, n.d.)

Affirmation

"I celebrate God with joy!"

Activity: Drawing

Draw a picture of what joy looks like to you when you think of God.

Day 3: Worshipping God Through Our Good Actions

Scripture

Romans 12:1: "Offer your bodies as a living sacrifice" (*Holy Bible NIV: New International Version*, n.d.).

Discussion

How can our everyday actions, like being kind or helping others, be a way to show our love and worship for God?

Activity: Challenge

Identify one act of kindness you can do today at school or at home.

Day 4: Worshipping God Sincerely

Scripture

John 4:24: "Worship in spirit and in truth" (*Holy Bible NIV: New International Version*, n.d.).

Prayer

Dear God,

Thank You for listening to my prayers. I am grateful for Your presence in my life and for the way You hear my hopes and struggles.

Teach me to worship You with a pure heart, free from distractions and filled with genuine love and gratitude. Help me to honor You in all that I do, and may my worship be a pleasing melody to You.

Amen.

Activity: Prayer

Write a prayer that comes from your heart.

Day 5: Praising God

God made the world and everything in it all very beautiful! When we take time to notice these amazing things around us, we show our appreciation for God's work. Worshiping God can be as simple as saying thank you for the beauty we see in nature or enjoying a sunny day. For example, we can spend time outside to remind us of how wonderful His creation is. By caring for the world and celebrating its beauty, we honor God and let Him know how much we love what He made!

Journaling

What are some of your favorite things in nature that remind you of God's beauty, and how can you show appreciation for His creation in your everyday life?

Scripture

Psalm 148:1: "Praise the Lord from the heavens; praise him in the heights above." (*Holy Bible NIV: New International Version*, n.d.).

Drawing

Draw a vibrant landscape featuring various elements of nature that reflect God's beautiful creation. Include colorful flowers, tall trees, a sparkling river, and a bright sun in the sky. Add animals like birds, butterflies, and deer, all celebrating together. In the foreground, illustrate children of different backgrounds joyfully praising God, with their arms raised, surrounded by the beauty of nature. Incorporate uplifting words or phrases like "Thank You, God!" or "Creation is Beautiful!" to emphasize the message of appreciation.

Activity: Sharing Opportunity

Organize a "Nature Praise Walk" where every member of the family can explore a nearby park, garden, or nature trail. Bring small notebooks and pencils to encourage each other to observe and write down or draw the beautiful things you see, such as flowers, trees, animals, and landscapes. After the walk, gather together and share one thing you found that reminded you of God's creation.

Day 6: Worshiping God Through Gratitude

Scripture

1 Thessalonians 5:18: "Give thanks in all circumstances" (*Holy Bible NIV: New International Version*, n.d.).

Affirmation

"I am thankful for all of God's blessings."

Activity: Challenge

Create a "Gratitude List" and share it with someone.

Day 7: End-Of-Week Review

- **Recap:** Discuss and share what you've learned from this week's topic with your family.
- **Scripture:** Matthew 18:20: "Where two or three gather in my name, there am I with them" (*Holy Bible NIV: New International Version*, n.d.).
- **Family Activity:** Plan a mini worship gathering with singing and prayers with family or friends.
- **Preparation for Next Week:** Wisdom is a precious gift that allows us to navigate the complexities of life with clarity and purpose. It begins with listening to God's guidance, as He speaks to us through His Word, prayer, and the gentle whispers of the Holy Spirit.

Week 23: Wisdom: Listening to God's Guidance

Day 1: What Is Wisdom?

Devotion

Wisdom is knowing what to do and making the right choices. God wants to guide us in all things!

In the ancient kingdom of Israel, there lived a young king named Solomon. He was known for his remarkable wisdom, a gift that had been bestowed upon him by God. After becoming king, Solomon sought to lead his people with fairness and understanding, knowing that wise choices would bring peace and prosperity to the land.

One day, two women came to Solomon with a deeply troubling dispute. Each woman claimed to be the mother of a baby, and they both wanted the child to be recognized as theirs. The court was filled with tension as each woman passionately pleaded her case, both insisting that the baby be given to her.

Solomon listened closely to both women, aware of the weight of the decision before him. Faced with this difficult situation, he needed to find a way to discern the truth. After a moment of contemplation, Solomon proposed a shocking solution. "Bring me a sword," he commanded.

The people were puzzled, but the sword was brought to him. "Since you both claim to be the mother, I will cut the baby in two and give each of you a half," Solomon declared.

At that moment, one of the women cried out in anguish, "Oh no, my lord! Please do not harm the child! Give her the baby instead! I would rather lose him than see him hurt!"

The other woman remained silent, her desire for the child overshadowed by her willingness to accept Solomon's decision. Seeing this, the king's heart was filled with understanding. He turned to the first woman and said, "You are the true mother! You have shown great love and compassion for your child. You deserve to keep him."

The court erupted in amazement. Solomon's wisdom had not only revealed the truth but had also saved the life of the innocent child. The people marveled at Solomon's ability to discern the right choice amid confusion and conflict.

Scripture

Proverbs 1:7: "The fear of the Lord is the beginning of knowledge" (*Holy Bible NIV: New International Version*, n.d.).

Activity

Reflect on your recent decision. What did you learn from it?

_____

_____

_____

_____

_____

_____

_____

Day 2: God Speaks to Us Through His Word

Reflection

How has reading the Bible provided me with guidance or wisdom in specific situations in my life, and what verses stand out as particularly impactful?

_____

_____

_____

_____

_____

_____

Scripture

Psalm 119:105: "Your word is a lamp to my feet and a light for my path" (*Holy Bible NIV: New International Version*, n.d.).

Affirmation

"God's word guides my decisions."

Activity: Challenge

Spend some time reading a Bible story and talk about it with someone.

Day 3: Asking God for Guidance

Scripture

James 1:5: "If any of you lacks wisdom, let him ask of God" (*Holy Bible NIV: New International Version*, n.d.).

Discussion

Why is it smart to ask for help when we need it, and how can praying to God guide us in making the right choices?

Activity: Challenge

Write a prayer asking God for wisdom in an area of your life.

_____

_____

_____

_____

_____

_____

_____

Day 4: Listening to Wise People

Scripture

Proverbs 12:15: "The way of fools seems right to them, but the wise listen to advice." (*Holy Bible NIV: New International Version*, n.d.).

Prayer

Dear Lord,

Help me to be open to advice and wise counsel. Teach me to listen carefully and discern truth from guidance, enabling me to grow and make sound decisions.

May I be receptive to learning and striving for wisdom in all areas of my life.

In Your Beautiful Name,

Amen.

Activity: Challenge

Talk with a trusted adult about a decision you need to make.

Day 5: Trusting God

Wisdom is like having a special flashlight that helps us see what's right and wrong in life. It helps us think carefully about our choices and actions. When we are wise, we can understand how our decisions affect ourselves and others. God's guidance is like a helpful map that shows us the best path to take. We can feel God guiding us to make good choices when we pray and listen. For example, if we have to decide whether to be helpful or selfish, wisdom helps us choose to be kind.

Journaling

Journal about a wise choice you made and why it was the right decision.

_____

_____

_____

_____

_____

_____

_____

Scripture

Proverbs 3:5-6: "Trust in the Lord with all your heart" (*Holy Bible NIV: New International Version*, n.d.).

Activity: Drawing

Draw a small boat with a child inside, sailing on calm waters with a guiding light or a star above, symbolizing God's guidance.

Day 6: Humility and Wisdom

Scripture

Proverbs 11:2: "When pride comes, then comes disgrace, but with humility comes wisdom" (*Holy Bible NIV: New International Version*, n.d.).

Affirmation

"I learn and grow every day."

Activity: Drawing

Create a drawing showing what wisdom looks like to you.

Day 7: End-Of-Week Review

- **Recap:** Discuss and share what you've learned from this week's topic with your family.
- **Scripture:** Psalm 37:4: "Delight yourself in the Lord" (*Holy Bible NIV: New International Version.*, n.d.).
- **Family Activity:** Explore nature while reflecting on God's wisdom and finding joy and peace in the journey. Create a list of items to find in nature that represent joy and peace (e.g., something green, something smooth, a flower, etc.). As you walk, encourage each family member to share

what they feel about following God's wisdom. Discuss how it helps you find joy and peace in life.

- **Preparation for Next Week:** God's love is the foundation of our faith. It is a love that knows no boundaries, reaching us in our highest joys and deepest struggles, assuring us that we are never alone. In moments of doubt or despair, we can find solace in the truth that God's love remains steadfast and unwavering, a constant source of hope and strength.

Week 24: God's Love: Unconditional and Everlasting

Day 1: Embraced by God's Love

Devotion

God's love is always with us, no matter what! Is there anything we can do to make Him love us more? No! His love is perfect.

 In a cozy little village, there lived a kind shepherd named Eli. Every day, Eli cared for his fluffy sheep, leading them to green pastures and flowing streams. Eli loved his sheep very much, and they loved him too!

One sunny afternoon, while counting his sheep, Eli realized that one little lamb had wandered away. "Oh no! Little Lily is missing!" he exclaimed. Without a second thought, Eli left the rest of his sheep in a safe place and went searching for Lily.

He called her name, "Lily! Where are you?" He climbed over hills, walked through grassy fields, and even crossed a small stream. Just when he was starting to feel worried, Eli heard a soft bleat coming from behind some bushes. He rushed over and found Lily stuck in a thorny bush, trembling and scared.

"Oh, sweet Lily! I've been looking for you!" Eli said as he gently untangled the thorns from her wool. "You don't have to be afraid; I'm here to take you home." As he picked her up and cradled her in his arms, Lily felt warm and safe.

Eli carried her all the way back to the flock, singing a joyful song. When they arrived, the other sheep bleated happily. Eli rejoiced, saying, "We must celebrate! I found my little lamb!"

Scripture

Romans 5:8: "But God shows his love for us in that while we were still sinners, Christ died for us" (*Holy Bible NIV: New International Version.*, n.d.).

Activity: Reflection

Reflect on ways you have felt God's love in your life.

___
___
___
___
___
___
___

Day 2: God's Love Is Everlasting

Reflection

How can I remind myself of the permanence of God's love during times of doubt or struggle?

___
___
___
___
___
___

Scripture

Jeremiah 31:3: "I have loved you with an everlasting love" (*Holy Bible NIV: New International Version*, n.d.).

Affirmation

"God's love lasts forever."

Activity: Art and Craft Project

Create a heart collage representing God's everlasting love.

Day 3: Loving Others

Scripture

1 John 4:19: "We love because he first loved us" (*Holy Bible NIV: New International Version.*, n.d.).

Discussion

What are some ways we can show God's love to others through our actions every day?

Activity: Challenge

Plan a kind act to do for a friend or family member.

Day 4: God Comforts Me

Scripture

Psalm 147:3: "He heals the brokenhearted and binds up their wounds" (*Holy Bible NIV: New International Version.*, n.d.).

Prayer

Dear God,

Thank You for being there for me, especially in hard times. Your unwavering support and love have brought me comfort and strength when I needed it most.

I am grateful for Your presence in my life, guiding me through challenges and helping me to persevere. May I continue to trust in Your goodness and find solace in Your embrace, knowing that I am never alone.

Amen.

Activity: Reflection

Write about a time when you felt comforted by God.

_____

_____

_____

_____

_____

_____

_____

Day 5: Loving Each Other

God's love is so big and amazing that it's meant for everyone, not just for us! When we show kindness, help our friends, or smile at someone, we are spreading God's love. We can also share love through our words by saying nice things or encouraging someone who feels sad. By being caring and loving, we make the world a happier place. Remember, the more love we share, the more it grows!

Journaling

How can I actively demonstrate God's love to those around me, and what specific actions can I take this week to spread His love to others in my community?

_____

_____

_____

_____

_____

_____

_____

Scripture

John 3:16: "For God so loved the world" (*Holy Bible NIV: New International Version.*, n.d.).

Activity: Drawing

Draw a picture of people from different backgrounds showing love to each other.

Day 6: Celebrating God

Scripture

Psalm 136:1: "Give thanks to the Lord, for he is good. His love endures forever" (*Holy Bible NIV: New International Version*, n.d.).

Affirmation

"I celebrate God's goodness and love."

Prayer

Thank you for all the good things in my life that show Your love, God!

Amen.

Activity

Create a "thankful list" of things you love about God.

Day 7: End-of-Week Review

- **Recap:** Discuss and share what you've learned from this week's topic with your family.
- **Scripture:** Ephesians 3:17-19: "May you have power... to grasp how wide and long and high and deep is the love of Christ" (*Holy Bible NIV: New International Version.*, n.d.).
- **Family Activity:** Host a small gathering to share stories of God's love with friends or family.
- **Preparation for Next Week:** By reflecting on God's words, we are transformed and equipped to face challenges with faith and share His love and truth with the world around us. The Bible is not just a book; it is a living testament of God's unfolding story and an invitation to learn, grow, and thrive in our spiritual walk.

Week 25: The Bible: Learning From God's Words

Day 1: Reading the Bible to Know God

Devotion

The Bible is God's special book for us. It's full of stories and lessons that help us understand Him better.

Once upon a time, in the ancient land of Israel, there lived a humble shepherd boy named Samuel. He was known for his kind heart and his love for God. Samuel spent many days tending to his father's sheep on the hills, but he always took time to listen to God's whispers in the quiet of the evening.

One day, as Samuel was resting under a great olive tree, he noticed a group of travelers passing by. They looked weary and worn from their journey. Samuel stood up and approached them with a smile. "Welcome, friends! What brings you to our village?" he asked.

The travelers replied, "We have come from a distant land to share an important message. We have brought with us a special book—the words of God that were given to His people."

Curiosity sparked in Samuel's heart. "A special book? What is it about?" he asked, eager to learn. The travelers smiled and explained, "This book contains the laws, stories, and promises of God. It is filled with wisdom, guidance, and comfort for everyone who seeks to know Him. It teaches us how to live in love and harmony with one another."

Samuel's eyes widened with wonder. "Can I see it?" he asked, stepping closer.

The travelers opened the book and began to read from it. They shared the stories of creation, the faith of Abraham, the bravery of Moses, and the love of David. As Samuel listened intently, he felt the warmth of God's presence wrapping around him. Each word seemed to fill his heart with joy and purpose.

"This is incredible!" Samuel exclaimed. "I want to learn more about God and His ways. Can I join you on your journey to spread these teachings?"

The travelers smiled with approval. "Of course, young shepherd. The Bible is God's special book for everyone, and it is meant to be shared. The more you learn and the more you share, the closer you will grow to God."

With that, Samuel set off with the travelers, eagerly absorbing the teachings of the Bible. He learned how to pray, how to trust in God's promises, and how to treat others with kindness. As they traveled from village to village, Samuel became a messenger of God's word, sharing the love and wisdom he had received.

Scripture

2 Timothy 3:16-17: "All scripture is God-breathed" (*Holy Bible NIV: New International Version*, n.d.).

Activity: Reflection

How has the Bible influenced your understanding of love, faith, and moral choices in your life?

_____

_____

_____

_____

_____

_____

_____

Day 2: The Bible Is My Source of Wisdom

Reflection

Which lessons from the Bible have most shaped how I live and treat others?

_____

_____

_____

_____

Scripture

Psalm 119:105: "Your word is a lamp to my feet" (*Holy Bible NIV: New International Version.*, n.d.).

Affirmation

"The Bible lights my path."

Activity: Drawing

Draw a picture of how the Bible shows you the way in life.

Day 3: Embracing God's Words

Scripture

Romans 15:4: "For everything that was written in the past was written to teach us" (*Holy Bible NIV: New International Version*, n.d.).

Discussion

How does reading the Bible help us learn more about God's love and what He wants for us, and why do you think every story in it matters?

Activity: Reflection

Write down one lesson you've learned from a Bible story.

_____

_____

_____

_____

_____

_____

Day 4: God's Words Provide Comfort and Hope

Scripture

Psalm 34:18: "The Lord is close to the brokenhearted" (*Holy Bible NIV: New International Version*, n.d.).

Prayer

Dear God,

Thank You for comforting me through Your word. I am grateful for the wisdom and strength that Your words provide. Help me to turn to You more often, finding solace in Your promises and guidance in Your teachings.

In Your Holy Name,

Amen.

Activity: Art and Craft Activity

Create a bookmark with your favorite comforting Bible verses on it.

Day 5: Discipleship

Sharing God's word means telling others about the teachings and stories we find in the Bible. It helps us learn more about God and His love for everyone. When we share what we've learned, we can inspire our friends and family to understand God better, too! This could be through talking about our favorite Bible stories, writing notes of encouragement, or even showing kindness to others. Sharing God's word helps spread joy and hope, and it brings us closer to each other.

Journaling

In what ways can I effectively share the lessons I've learned from the Bible with others, and how can I encourage them to explore God's word in their own lives?

_____

_____

_____

_____

_____

_____

_____

Scripture

Matthew 28:19: "Go therefore and make disciples" (*Holy Bible NIV: New International Version*, n.d.).

Activity: Drawing

Create a drawing of a large, colorful tree with its branches filled with leaves shaped like open books, each with a Bible verse written on it. Add yourself reading or sharing with others.

Day 6: Asking Questions

Scripture

Proverbs 18:15: "The heart of the discerning acquires knowledge" (*Holy Bible NIV: New International Version*, n.d.).

Affirmation

"I ask questions to learn more."

Activity: Challenge

Write down questions you have about God or the Bible and discuss them with a trusted adult.

_____
_____
_____
_____
_____
_____
_____

Day 7: End-Of-Week Review

- **Recap:** Discuss and share what you've learned from this week's topic with your family.
- **Scripture:** John 15:15: "I have called you friends" (*Holy Bible NIV: New International Version*, n.d.).

- **Family Activity:** Create a "Friendship with God" journal where you can write prayers and thoughts.
- **Preparation of Next Week:** The Holy Spirit serves as our divine Helper and Guide, constantly at work in our lives to lead us toward truth, understanding, and comfort. Through His presence, we receive wisdom in our moments of confusion, strength in our times of weakness, and encouragement when we face life's challenges.

Week 26: The Holy Spirit: Our Helper and Guide

Day 1: The Holy Spirit Helps You

Devotion

The Holy Spirit is God's special helper. He guides us in making good choices and comforts us when we're sad.

In the bustling city of Jerusalem, there lived a young woman named Mary. Mary was known for her kind heart and her unwavering faith in God. She spent her days caring for her family and helping her neighbors, always striving to make good choices.

One evening, as the sun began to set, Mary joined a gathering of followers of Jesus. They were discussing the recent events that had taken place, including Jesus' miracles, His teachings, and the sadness they felt after His crucifixion. Mary listened intently, her heart heavy with sorrow, yet full of faith.

Just as they were speaking, a man named Peter stood up and recalled Jesus' promise to them: "Do not be afraid, for I will send you a Helper, the Holy Spirit. He will guide you and remind you of all that I have taught you."

The mention of the Holy Spirit sparked a flicker of hope in Mary's heart. She had heard the stories of how the Holy Spirit would bring comfort and guidance to those in need, and she longed for that support.

As days turned into weeks, Mary and the other followers gathered often to pray and seek guidance. Then, one day, on the day of Pentecost, everything changed. Suddenly, a sound like a mighty rushing wind filled the room, and flames appeared, resting on each person present. It was the Holy Spirit arriving—God's special helper had come!

The Holy Spirit filled each of them with courage and strength. They began to speak in different languages, sharing the good news of Jesus with everyone around them. Mary felt a surge of joy and peace within her. The Holy Spirit was guiding her actions, helping her to make good choices and encouraging her to share God's love.

In the days that followed, Mary encountered challenges. There were times when she felt sadness and doubt creeping into her heart, especially as they faced opposition to their faith. Yet, during those moments, she would pray, and the Holy Spirit would comfort her like a warm embrace. Mary would feel a gentle whisper in her heart reminding her of God's promises and the power she held through faith.

As Mary spoke, she felt the Holy Spirit guiding her words. Leah's eyes filled with tears, and for the first time since her loss, she felt a flicker of hope igniting in her heart.

Over time, Mary continued to rely on the Holy Spirit for guidance in her life and to bring comfort to others. She realized that the Holy Spirit was not just a distant promise but a living presence that offered wisdom, courage, and peace.

Scripture

John 14:26: "But the Helper, the Holy Spirit, whom the Father will send in my name, he will teach you all things" (*Holy Bible NIV: New International Version*, n.d.).

Activity: Reflection

Reflect on a time when you felt the Holy Spirit helping you. Write about it.

_____

_____

_____

_____

_____

_____

_____

Day 2: The Holy Spirit Always Listens to Us

Reflection

How can I build a closer, friendlier connection with the Holy Spirit through my prayers, and what particular thoughts or worries do I want to share with Him?

_____

_____

_____

_____

_____

_____

_____

Scripture

Romans 8:26: "The Spirit helps us in our weakness" (*Holy Bible NIV: New International Version*, n.d.).

Affirmation

"I can talk to the Holy Spirit anytime."

Activity: Prayer

Spend a few minutes in silent prayer, listening for the Holy Spirit.

Day 3: I Am Brave and Strong With the Holy Spirit by My Side

Scripture

Acts 1:8: "But you will receive power when the Holy Spirit has come upon you" (*Holy Bible NIV: New International Version*, n.d.).

Discussion

How does the Holy Spirit help us find the strength and courage to do good things, especially when we're feeling scared or unsure?

Activity: Challenge

Identify a challenge you face and write down how you can rely on the Holy Spirit for help.

_____
_____
_____
_____
_____
_____
_____
_____

Day 4: The Holy Spirit Teaches Me About God

Scripture

John 16:13: "When the Spirit of truth comes, he will guide you into all the truth" (*Holy Bible NIV: New International Version*, n.d.).

Prayer

Dear Lord,

Thank You for teaching me through the Holy Spirit. I am grateful for the guidance, wisdom, and understanding that You provide.

Help me to be receptive to the lessons and insights imparted by the Spirit, enabling me to grow in faith and maturity.

In Your Holy Name,

Amen.

Activity: Challenge

Choose a Bible verse and discuss what it means with a friend or family member.

Day 5: Trusting the Holy Spirit

It can be hard to know what to do when we feel lost or confused. The Holy Spirit is like a special helper God gives us to guide us. It helps us feel calm and think clearly, showing us the right choices to make. For example, the Holy Spirit can remind us to be kind if we're unsure whether to help a friend or ignore them. We can find the right path by listening to that little voice in our hearts.

Reflection

How can we ask the Holy Spirit for help when we're feeling lost or confused, and how can we listen for His guidance to make the right choices?

_____

_____

_____

_____

_____

_____

_____

Scripture

Psalm 32:8: "I will instruct you and teach you in the way you should go" (*Holy Bible NIV: New International Version*, n.d.).

Activity: Drawing

Draw a scene of a child standing at a crossroads, looking unsure. Above them, depict a bright light or a dove symbolizing the Holy Spirit, shining down and illuminating a path. On one side of the drawing, illustrate fun and safe choices (like helping a friend or reading the Bible); on the other side, show confusing or unwise choices (like being mean or ignoring good advice).

Day 6: The Fruits of the Spirit

Scripture

Galatians 5:22-23: "But the fruit of the Spirit is love, joy, peace, forbearance, kindness..." (*Holy Bible NIV: New International Version*, n.d.).

Affirmation

"I show the fruits of the Spirit in my life."

Activity: Drawing

Draw or create a fruit basket that represents the fruits of the Spirit, coloring each fruit with a different quality.

Day 7: Sharing God's Love

- **Recap:** Discuss and share what you've learned from this week's topic with your family.
- **Scripture:** Matthew 28:19: "Go therefore and make disciples of all nations..." (*Holy Bible NIV: New International Version*, n.d.).
- **Family Activity:** With your family, plan a way to share a positive message or kindness with others in your community this week.
- **Preparation for Next Week:** Being part of God's family through community is a profound blessing that reflects the heart of Christ's teachings. Within this sacred family, we discover the power of connection, support, and love as we gather together in faith to encourage one another on our spiritual journeys.

Week 27: Community: Being Part of God's Family

Day 1: Caring for Each Other

Devotion

Being part of God's family means we support and care for each other—just like brothers and sisters!

In a modest village nestled at the foot of a great mountain, there lived a diverse group of people who called themselves the Family of Hope. They were united not by blood but by faith and a shared understanding of being part of God's family. Each member was different—some were young, others old, some were strong, and others were frail—but all were cherished.

One day, the village received word that a terrible storm was approaching. The sky darkened, and a sense of urgency filled the air. The elders gathered to discuss how they could prepare. Among them was a woman named Hannah, known for her wisdom and grace. She reminded them, "In times of trouble, we must look to one another. Being part of God's family means supporting each other."

With her guidance, they set to work. Families banded together; the strong helped the weak, and those with knowledge of construction shared their skills. They fortified homes, ensuring everyone had enough food and shelter. As the storm drew nearer, the village became a flurry of activity.

When the storm finally hit, it howled like a wild beast, rattling windows and whipping through the streets. But inside the homes, the villagers were together. They gathered in communal spaces, sharing meals and stories and singing songs of hope. The children played games, bringing laughter into the somber night.

When morning came and the sun broke through the clouds, the village emerged to assess the damage. Many homes were damaged, but no one was alone. The Family of Hope came together, sharing tools, skills, and love. They worked side by side, supporting one another and rebuilding what had been lost.

Scripture

Ephesians 2:19: "So then you are no longer strangers, but fellow citizens with the saints" (*Holy Bible NIV: New International Version*, n.d.).

Activity: Reflection

Reflect on how your church or family supports you.

___

Day 2: Using My Gifts

Journaling

Write down your gifts and how you can use them in your community.

___

Scripture

1 Corinthians 12:12: "For just as the body is one and has many members" (*Holy Bible NIV: New International Version*, n.d.).

Affirmation

"I use my gifts to help my family and friends."

Activity: Challenge

Organize small group discussions where kids can share their spiritual gifts. Encourage them to talk about how they feel their gifts can be used to help others and seek ways to collaborate on projects.

Day 3: Encouraging One Another

Scripture

Hebrews 10:24-25: "Let us consider how we may spur one another on toward love and good deeds" (*Holy Bible NIV: New International Version*, n.d.).

Discussion

With your family, discuss how we can encourage each other in daily life.

Activity: Challenge

Write a note of encouragement to someone you know.

Day 4: Loving Everyone

Scripture

John 13:34: "A new command I give you: Love one another" (*Holy Bible NIV: New International Version*, n.d.).

Prayer

Dear God,

Thank You for loving me just as I am. Help me learn to love everyone around me, even when they are different.

Teach me to see the good in others and to be kind and friendly to everyone I meet. Thank You for making all of us unique and special.

In Your Beautiful Name,

Amen.

Activity: Challenge

Start a prayer chain where you and your friends pray for each other.

Day 5: Supporting Those in Need

When we or our friends face challenges, like feeling sad or struggling with school, it's good to be there for one another. We can pray for each other, which means talking to God and asking for His help and comfort. Helping can also be as simple as listening, sharing a kind word, or doing something nice, like making a card. When we support our friends, it shows we care and makes them feel loved. Helping one another can turn tough times into moments of friendship and hope.

Reflection

How can I help others carry their burdens, and what practical steps can I take to show kindness and support to those who are struggling?

_____

_____

_____

_____

_____

_____

_____

Scripture

Galatians 6:2: "Carry each other's burdens" (*Holy Bible NIV: New International Version*, n.d.).

Activity: Drawing

Draw a picture or create a craft that represents your love for each other

Day 6: Feeling Joyful for My Community

Scripture

Philippians 1:3: "I thank my God every time I remember you" (*Holy Bible NIV: New International Version*, n.d.).

Affirmation

"I celebrate joy in our community."

Activity: Challenge

Organize a small gathering or game day with your family or friends.

Day 7: End-Of-Week Review

- **Recap:** Discuss and share what you've learned from this week's topic with your family.
- **Scripture:** 1 Peter 4:10: "Each of you should use whatever gift you have received to serve others" (*Holy Bible NIV: New International Version*, n.d.).
- **Family Activity:** Plan or participate in a community service project with your family.
- **Preparation for Next Week:** When we take the time to reflect on God's goodness, we are reminded of His grace, which sustains us through life's challenges, and His mercy, which forgives our mistakes.

Week 28: Celebrating God's Goodness

Day 1: God Is Good

Devotion

God is very good, and we can see it in everything around us! Celebrating His goodness helps us remember His blessings.

Once upon a time, in a beautiful garden called Eden, God created the world and everything in it. He filled it with stunning flowers, towering trees, colorful birds, and gentle animals. Each day, God looked at His creations and smiled, saying, "It is good!"

One sunny afternoon, a little girl named Lily played in her backyard. She loved to explore the flowers and listen to the cheerful songs of the birds. As she ran through the garden, she spotted her neighbor, Mr. Thomas, the gardener. He was tending to his plants, making them grow tall and strong.

"Hello, Mr. Thomas!" Lily called out. "How do you make your flowers so beautiful?"

Mr. Thomas smiled kindly and replied, "Lily, it's all about caring for them and remembering to celebrate their beauty. Just like God cares for us and all His creations!"

Curious, Lily asked, "How can we celebrate God's goodness?"

Mr. Thomas thought for a moment and said, "Well, look around you! We can see God's goodness in the bright sun shining down, the soft breeze blowing, and the flowers dancing. Every time we appreciate these blessings, we celebrate Him!"

Scripture

Psalm 100:5: "For the Lord is good and his love endures forever" (*Holy Bible NIV: New International Version*, n.d.).

Activity: Reflection

Make a list of five things you are grateful for and thank God for them.

_____
_____
_____
_____
_____
_____
_____

Day 2: Being Thankful

Scripture

1 Thessalonians 5:18: "Give thanks in all circumstances" (*Holy Bible NIV: New International Version*, n.d.).

Affirmation

"I am thankful for God's blessings."

Activity: Challenge

Write a thank-you note to someone who has been a blessing in your life.

Day 3: God Loves Everyone

Scripture

Psalm 145:9: "The Lord is good to all" (*Holy Bible NIV: New International Version*, n.d.).

Discussion

Discuss with your family how God's goodness is not only for us but also for everyone around us.

Activity: Challenge

Plan a way to perform an act of kindness for someone else today.

Day 4: Singing to the Lord

Scripture

Psalm 98:1: "Sing to the Lord a new song, for he has done marvelous things" (*Holy Bible NIV: New International Version*, n.d.).

Prayer

Dear God,

Thank You for the wonderful gift of music and the joy it brings to our hearts. I am grateful for the opportunity to sing praises to You, celebrating Your greatness and love.

May my voice bring joy to others and honor You in all that I do.

Amen.

Activity: Music

Create a song about something good God has done in your life.

Day 5: Sharing God's Goodness

Sharing stories about God's goodness is a wonderful way to inspire others and spread happiness! When we talk about the amazing things God has done in our lives, like helping us when we were sad or answering our prayers, it can give hope to our friends. When we share these experiences, we encourage others to trust God, too! So, let's remember to tell our family and friends about the good things God is doing, whether big or small.

Journaling

How can I share a story about God's goodness in my life with someone, and what impact do I hope it will have on them?

_____

_____

_____

_____

_____

_____

_____

Scripture

Psalm 71:15: "My mouth will tell of your righteous deeds" (*Holy Bible NIV: New International Version*, n.d.).

Activity: Drawing

Draw a scene showing how God has been good to you.

Day 6: Acknowledging God's Goodness

Scripture

Lamentations 3:22-23: "His mercies are new every morning" (*Holy Bible NIV: New International Version*, n.d.).

Affirmation

"I notice God's goodness each day."

Activity: Journaling

Create a "Goodness Journal" where you write down things that remind you of God's goodness each day.

Day 7: End-Of-Week Review

- **Recap:** Discuss and share what you've learned from this week's topic with your family.
- **Scripture:** Psalm 145:7: "They celebrate your abundant goodness" (*Holy Bible NIV: New International Version*, n.d.).
- **Family Activity:** Host a small gathering with friends and family to celebrate God's goodness, sharing food and blessings.
- **Preparation for Next Week:** Jesus exemplified compassion throughout His ministry, healing the sick, feeding the hungry, and offering solace to the broken-hearted. As we open our hearts to those in need, we participate in God's work, becoming vessels of His grace and mercy in the world.

Week 29: Compassion: Caring for Those in Need

Day 1: What Is Compassion?

Devotion

Compassion means caring for others, especially when they are hurt or sad. We can show kindness as God shows compassion to us.

Once upon a time, in a bustling town called Jericho, there lived a man who was traveling down a dusty road. As he walked, he was suddenly attacked by robbers who took his money and left him hurt and alone by the side of the road.

Later, a priest walked by. When he saw the hurt man, he crossed to the other side of the road and hurried past without helping. Then, a Levite, who also served in the temple, came down the same road. He saw the man lying there but chose to ignore him and continued on his way.

But then, a Samaritan—a man from a group that often did not get along with the Jews—came down the road. When he saw the injured man, his heart filled with compassion. Unlike the others, the Samaritan stopped to help. He knelt beside the man, bandaged his wounds, and even helped him onto his donkey.

The kind Samaritan took the man to an inn, where he cared for him. He paid the innkeeper to take good care of the injured man, saying, "Whenever you need more money for his care, I will come back and pay you."

Just like the Samaritan showed kindness to someone in need, we can show compassion, too. We can help our friends when they are feeling down, share a smile with someone who is lonely, or lend a hand to others who are struggling.

Scripture

Colossians 3:12: "As God's chosen people, clothe yourselves with compassion" (*Holy Bible NIV: New International Version*, n.d.).

Affirmation

"I care for others with compassion."

Activity: Reflection

Reflect on someone in need around you and think of how you can help them.

_____

_____

_____

_____

_____

_____

_____

Day 2: Being Compassionate

Scripture

Matthew 14:14: "When Jesus landed and saw a large crowd, he had compassion on them" (*Holy Bible NIV: New International Version*, n.d.).

Affirmation

"I help those who are in need."

Activity: Challenge

Write down ways to help someone in your community, like volunteering or donating items.

_____

_____

_____

_____

_____

_____

_____

_____

Day 3: Understanding Others' Feelings

Discussion

Discuss why compassion involves understanding and feeling for others. When we see others sad, our hearts should want to help them feel better.

Scripture

Romans 12:15: "Rejoice with those who rejoice; mourn with those who mourn" (*Holy Bible NIV: New International Version*, n.d.).

Activity: Challenge

Practice active listening with a friend today, noticing how they feel.

Day 4: Sharing Kind Words

Scripture

Proverbs 12:25: "Anxiety weighs down the heart, but a kind word cheers it up" (*Holy Bible NIV: New International Version*, n.d.).

Prayer

Dear God,

Please help me to share kind words with those who need them. Encourage me to be present whenever they need me.

Let my heart be open to uplifting others with my words.

In Your Holy Name,

Amen.

Activity: Challenge

Write and give someone a heartfelt compliment.

Day 5: Practicing Compassion Each Day

Compassion is about feeling kindness and wanting to help when we see someone in need. It's like when we notice a friend who is sad, and we want to cheer them up. When we act on that feeling and do something to help, we show compassion! We can help by sharing, being a good listener, or even volunteering our time to help people in our community. Every small act of kindness matters!

Journaling

How can I actively demonstrate compassion in my daily life to help those in need, following the example of Jesus?

_____

_____

_____

_____

_____

Scripture

1 John 3:18: "Let us not love with words or speech, but with actions and in truth" (*Holy Bible NIV: New International Version*, n.d.).

Activity: Drawing

Draw a colorful garden scene where children are helping each other plant flowers and veggies.

Day 6: Supporting Others With Compassion

Scripture

Galatians 6:2: "Carry each other's burdens" (*Holy Bible NIV: New International Version*, n.d.).

Affirmation

"I support my community with compassion."

Activity: Art and Craft Project

Create a collage that represents inclusivity and compassion in your community using pictures or words.

Day 7: End-Of-Week Review

- **Recap:** Discuss and share what you've learned from this week's topic with your family.
- **Scripture:** Luke 10:37: "Go and do likewise" (*Holy Bible NIV: New International Version*, n.d.).
- **Family Activity:** Organize or participate in a community service project, like cleaning up a park or food drive.
- **Preparation for Next Week:** We are not defined by our past mistakes, worldly achievements, or the opinions of others; instead, our true identity is rooted in being beloved children of God. In Christ, we are redeemed, accepted, and made new, called to embrace the unique purpose He has for each of us.

Week 30: Identity in Christ: Understanding Who We Are

Day 1: Our True Identity

Devotion

Our true identity comes from being a child of God. We are loved, special, and important to Him!

Once upon a time, a young girl named Lydia lived in a small village. Despite being surrounded by laughter and friends, Lydia often felt alone and unworthy. She often compared herself to the other children, believing she wasn't as talented or loved. While wandering near the river one day, she met an elderly woman named Miriam who radiated warmth and kindness.

Seeing Lydia's troubled expression, Miriam invited her to sit by the water. With a gentle voice, she shared stories about how God created each person uniquely, emphasizing that everyone is special in His eyes. Miriam spoke of how even the smallest bird in the sky is cared for by God and how much more He cherishes each of His children.

Moved by these words, Lydia asked, "Do you really think I'm special, too?" Miriam smiled and placed her hand on Lydia's shoulder. "Absolutely, my dear! Your true identity comes from being a child of God. You are loved beyond measure, and He has a wonderful plan just for you."

Scripture

1 John 3:1: "See what great love the Father has lavished on us, that we should be called children of God!" (*Holy Bible NIV: New International Version*, n.d.)

Affirmation

"I am a child of God."

Activity: Challenge

Write a poem or song about being a child of God.

_____

_____

_____

_____

_____

_____

Day 2: Being Renewed

Scripture

2 Corinthians 5:17: "Therefore, if anyone is in Christ, the new creation has come" (*Holy Bible NIV: New International Version*, n.d.).

Affirmation

"I am a new creation in Christ."

Activity: Reflection

Reflect on what it means to be a child of God. Write or draw about it in a journal.

_____

_____

_____

Day 3: Redemption

Discussion

Discuss how our identity in Christ means we are forgiven and free. We don't have to carry our mistakes or guilt.

Scripture

Ephesians 1:7: "In him, we have redemption through his blood" (*Holy Bible NIV: New International Version*, n.d.).

Activity: Challenge

List some things you need to let go of and pray for forgiveness.

Day 4: God Has Plans for Me

Scripture

Jeremiah 29:11: "For I know the plans I have for you" (*Holy Bible NIV: New International Version*, n.d.).

Prayer

Dear God,

Reveal to me the plans You have for my life. Guide my steps and help me trust in Your perfect timing.

Amen.

Activity: Challenge

Write down your dreams and what you believe God is calling you to do.

_____

_____

_____

_____

_____

_____

_____

Day 5: We Are Part of God's Family

In Christ, we are all equal and loved by God! This means that it doesn't matter where we come from, what we look like, or what we have; everyone is special and precious in God's eyes. When we believe in Jesus, we become part of a big family called God's family. Just like a family, we love and support each other. We celebrate our differences because they make us unique!

Reflection

What does it mean to be part of God's Family?

_____
_____
_____
_____
_____
_____
_____

Scripture

Galatians 3:28: "There is neither Jew nor Gentile, neither slave nor free, nor is there male and female, for you are all one in Christ Jesus" (*Holy Bible NIV: New International Version*, n.d.).

Activity: Art and Craft Activity

Create a visual representation of unity within your community, like a mural or collage.

Day 6: Being God's Light

Scripture

Matthew 5:14: "You are the light of the world" (*Holy Bible NIV: New International Version*, n.d.).

Affirmation

"I shine God's light."

Activity: Drawing

Draw an image of a light, symbolizing your role as a light in the world.

Day 7: End-Of-Week Review

- **Recap:** Discuss and share what you've learned from this week's topic with your family.
- **Scripture:** 1 Peter 2:9: "But you are a chosen people, a royal priesthood" (*Holy Bible NIV: New International Version*, n.d.).
- **Family Activity:** Host a celebration gathering with friends or family focusing on identity in Christ—share stories and encouragement!
- **Preparation for Next Week:** Church is not merely a place for worship but a sanctuary where we can learn from one another, deepening our understanding of God's Word and His purpose for our lives.

Week 31: The Importance of Church: Gathering to Grow

Day 1: Going to Church

Devotion

Going to church is important because it helps us learn about God and grow in our faith. It's a place to worship together!

In the bustling town of Bethany, the sun rose over the hills, casting a golden glow on a small, humble church nestled at the center of the village. It was Sunday, and families filled the streets, making their way to worship. Among them was a young boy named Samuel, who was eager to attend church with his parents.

As they entered the church, Samuel was greeted by the warm smiles of the congregation. The air was filled with joyful hymns as the community gathered to worship together. Samuel's heart swelled with excitement; he loved hearing the stories of God's love and learning about the teachings of Jesus. Today, the pastor was going to share the parable of the lost sheep, a story Samuel had heard before but never grew tired of.

As the sermon began, Samuel listened intently, absorbing every word. He learned how, just like a shepherd cares for each sheep, God cherishes every one of His children. The pastor emphasized the importance of community, explaining that gathering in church allowed them to support one another and grow in their faith together. Samuel felt encouraged by the message, understanding that he was not alone on his journey.

After the service, the congregation mingled, sharing laughter and stories. Samuel noticed an older man, Mr. Jacobs, who seemed lonely. Remembering the pastor's words about caring for one another, Samuel approached him with a big smile and asked if he would like to join him for lunch. Mr. Jacobs' face lit up with gratitude, and together they shared a meal filled with joy and friendship.

Scripture

Hebrews 10:24-25: "And let us consider how we may spur one another on toward love and good deeds, not giving up meeting together" (*Holy Bible NIV: New International Version*, n.d.).

Activity: Challenge

Write a note or card to someone in your church, thanking them for being a part of your life.

Day 2: Being Part of My Community

Scripture

1 Corinthians 12:12: "For just as the body is one and has many members" (*Holy Bible NIV: New International Version*, n.d.).

Affirmation

"I belong to a caring community."

Activity: Drawing

Reflect on what you enjoy most about going to church and draw a picture of it.

_____
_____
_____
_____
_____
_____
_____

Day 3: Hearing the Words of God

Discussion

Discuss how we can learn about God's word through lessons, songs, and fellowship.

Scripture

Romans 10:17: "So faith comes from hearing, and hearing through the word of Christ" (*Holy Bible NIV: New International Version*, n.d.).

Activity: Challenge

Choose a Bible story you learned about in church to retell to a family member or friend.

Day 4: Worship Through Songs

Scripture

Psalm 100:2: "Worship the Lord with gladness; come before him with joyful songs" (*Holy Bible NIV: New International Version*, n.d.).

Prayer

Dear Lord,

Help me to worship You with all my heart. Teach me to sing joyfully, to pray sincerely, and to show my love through all that I do.

May my heart be filled with Your joy, as I celebrate Your goodness and grace.

In Your Beautiful Name,

Amen.

Activity: Singing

Sing your favorite worship song and encourage family or friends to join you.

Day 5: Serving Others With Joy

Serving others through the church is a special way we can show God's love in action! When we help people, like volunteering for events, donating food, or visiting those who are lonely, we are sharing kindness and making a difference in our community. Helping others is a big part of church life because it shows that we care about everyone, just like God cares for us. When we work together as a church family to serve, we create joy and bring people closer.

Reflection

Why is serving others through the church a way we can show God's love in action?

_____

_____

_____

_____

_____

_____

_____

Scripture

Galatians 5:13: "Serve one another humbly in love" (*Holy Bible NIV: New International Version*, n.d.).

Activity: Drawing

Create a drawing that represents a colorful scene of children joyfully singing and dancing in a church or open field, with musical notes floating in the air.

Day 6: I'm Safe and Accepted in My Community

Scripture

Colossians 3:12: "Therefore, as God's chosen people, clothe yourselves with compassion, kindness..." (*Holy Bible NIV: New International Version*, n.d.).

Affirmation

"I feel safe and accepted in my church family."

Activity

Reflect on a time someone in your church helped you or made you feel special. Write about it in your journal.

Day 7: End-Of-Week Review

- **Recap:** Discuss and share what you've learned from this week's topic with your family.
- **Scripture:** Matthew 18:20: "For where two or three gather in my name, there am I with them" (*Holy Bible NIV: New International Version*, n.d.).
- **Family Activity:** Create a prayer wall or jar at home where you and your family can write down prayer requests for your church.

- **Preparation for Next Week:** Just as we get excited about a new toy, a great book, or a fun game, we can also share the best news ever—the news that God loves everyone and that, through Jesus, we can always be close to Him. When we share the Gospel, we open the door for others to know how special they are to God and how they can experience His love and joy in their lives.

Week 32: Sharing the Gospel: Telling Others About Jesus

Day 1: The Gospel

Devotion

Sharing the good news about Jesus is important! We can tell others about His love and what He has done for us.

In a small village by the Sea of Galilee, there lived a young girl named Naomi. She was known for her bright smile and sparkling eyes, and everyone in the village loved her. One day, after spending time with her family, Naomi learned about Jesus and the incredible stories of His love and miracles from the fishermen who had seen Him teach the crowds.

Filled with excitement, Naomi felt an overwhelming desire to share the good news about Jesus with her friends. She remembered how the fishermen spoke about the time Jesus calmed the storm and how He healed the sick. With a heart full of hope, she gathered her friends at the edge of the sea to tell them all the amazing things she had learned.

"Listen, everyone! I have something wonderful to share!" she exclaimed, her voice bright with enthusiasm. Her friends gathered around, curious about what Naomi had to say. "There's this man named Jesus who loves us so much! He helps those who are hurting, makes the blind see, and even calms the wildest storms!"

As she shared these stories, her friends listened eagerly, their eyes wide with wonder. Naomi told them how Jesus cared for everyone, especially those who felt lonely or sad. She spoke about how He forgives mistakes and offers us a chance to start fresh.

Inspired by Naomi's passion, her friends began to ask questions, eager to learn more. Naomi warmly welcomed their inquiries, explaining how they, too, could talk to Jesus in prayer and invite Him into their hearts. She said, "We can share His love with everyone, just like a candle that shines brightly in the darkness!"

That day, Naomi and her friends promised each other that they would share the good news about Jesus with others in their village. They began telling their families, helping those in need, and inviting more friends to join them in learning about Jesus' love.

Scripture

Mark 16:15: "Go into all the world and proclaim the gospel to the whole creation" (*Holy Bible NIV: New International Version*, n.d.).

Activity: Challenge

Think of a friend or family member you'd like to tell about Jesus. Write a note or message to share with them.

Day 2: Shining My Light

Scripture

Matthew 5:16: "Let your light shine before others..." (*Holy Bible NIV: New International Version*, n.d.).

Affirmation

"I shine my light for Jesus."

Activity: Challenge

Write a list of ways you can show kindness to others.

_____

_____

_____

_____

_____

_____

_____

Day 3: Sharing the Teachings of Jesus

Discussion

Discuss why everyone needs to hear about Jesus. We can share the gospel with our friends, family, and even people we meet!

Scripture

Acts 1:8: "You will be my witnesses in Jerusalem..." (*Holy Bible NIV: New International Version*, n.d.).

Activity: Art and Craft Project

Create a "love wall" showcasing pictures of different cultures and people, celebrating diversity.

Day 4: Jesus' Love Is Unconditional

Scripture

John 3:16: "For God so loved the world..." (*Holy Bible NIV: New International Version*, n.d.).

Prayer

Dear Lord,

Teach me to love everyone just like You do. Help me to be kind and show compassion and to see the good in all my friends and family.

May my heart be a reflection of Your love.

In Jesus' Name,

Amen.

Activity: Challenge

Choose a Bible verse that is meaningful to you and share it with someone.

Day 5: Declaring God's Glory

Sharing the gospel means talking about the good news of Jesus! It can be super simple and fun. One way to share is by telling someone what Jesus means to you, like how He makes you feel loved and happy. You could say, "Jesus is my friend, and He helps me be brave!" Another way is to share a special Bible verse, which is like a treasure of wisdom. You might say, "I love this verse that says, 'God is with you always!'" Sharing these messages can inspire others and help them learn about God's love.

Journaling

How can I share my favorite Bible verse or a personal story about Jesus with someone this week?

_____
_____
_____
_____
_____
_____
_____

Scripture

Psalm 96:3: "Declare his glory among the nations" (*Holy Bible NIV: New International Version*, n.d.).

Activity: Drawing

Draw a world map and mark places you'd like to reach with the gospel.

Day 6: Inviting Others to Learn About Jesus

Scripture

Luke 14:23: "Go out to the highways and hedges and compel people to come in..." (*Holy Bible NIV: New International Version*, n.d.).

Affirmation

"I invite others to know Jesus."

Activity: Challenge

Create invitations to a church event or youth group to give to friends.

Day 7: End-Of-Week Review

- **Recap:** Discuss and share what you've learned from this week's topic with your family.
- **Scripture:** Colossians 4:3: "Pray for us, too, that God may open a door for our message" (*Holy Bible NIV: New International Version*, n.d.).

- **Family Activity:** Create a prayer list of people you want to share the gospel with and commit to praying for them regularly.
- **Preparation for Next Week:** The Beatitudes are special teachings from Jesus that show us how to live a blessed and happy life! They are found in the Bible during the Sermon on the Mount, where Jesus shares important lessons about kindness, love, and being humble. Let's dive in and explore how living the blessed life can make a big difference in our hearts and in the lives of those we meet!

Week 33: The Beatitudes: Living the Blessed Life

Day 1: The Beatitudes

Devotion

The Beatitudes teach us about how to live a blessed life. They remind us that we are blessed when we care for others.

One sunny afternoon in the small town of Maplewood, a young boy named Ethan was playing in the park when he noticed a little girl sitting alone on a bench, quietly watching the other children play. Her name was Lily, and Ethan could see that she looked sad and left out. Remembering the Beatitudes he had learned about in Sunday school, which taught him that those who are kind and help others are truly blessed, Ethan felt a nudge in his heart.

With a smile, he approached Lily and asked, "Would you like to play with us?" Lily's eyes brightened, and she nodded shyly. Ethan took her hand and led her to the group playing tag. As they ran and laughed together, Ethan felt a warm glow inside, knowing he was living out the teachings of the Beatitudes by caring for someone in need.

By the end of the day, Lily was beaming with happiness, and their new friendship blossomed. Through this little act of love, he understood that the Beatitudes were not just words but a way to live a truly blessed life.

Scripture

Matthew 5:3: "Blessed are the poor in spirit, for theirs is the kingdom of heaven" (*Holy Bible NIV: New International Version*, n.d.).

Activity: Reflection

Reflect on how humility affects your life. Write your thoughts.

_____

_____

_____

_____

_____

_____

_____

Day 2: Comforting Others

Scripture

Matthew 5:4: "Blessed are those who mourn, for they will be comforted" (*Holy Bible NIV: New International Version*, n.d.).

Affirmation

"I bring comfort to those who are sad."

Activity: Challenge

Think of someone who needs comfort and write them a supportive note.

Day 3: Being Gentle and Kind

Discussion

Discuss how God wants us to be gentle and kind. We can show this in our actions and words.

Scripture

Matthew 5:5: "Blessed are the meek, for they will inherit the earth" (*Holy Bible NIV: New International Version*, n.d.).

Activity: Challenge

Make a "Kindness Jar" where you can drop in ideas of kind things you can do for others.

Day 4: Doing What's Right

Scripture

Matthew 5:6: "Blessed are those who hunger and thirst for righteousness" (*Holy Bible NIV: New International Version*, n.d.).

Prayer

Dear God,

Help me to always choose what is right and good. Give me the wisdom to make the best choices and the courage to stand up for what I believe.

In Jesus' Name,

Amen.

Activity

Journal about a time when you stood up for what was right.

_____

_____

_____

_____

_____

_____

_____

Day 5: Being Merciful

Being merciful means being really kind and forgiving to others, even when they make mistakes. It's like when a friend accidentally bumps into you; instead of getting angry, you forgive them and say it's okay. When we show mercy, we're acting like God because He is so loving and forgiving toward us! Showing mercy can be helping someone who needs it, saying nice things, or understanding when someone is having a tough day.

Reflection

Why does being merciful mean being kind and forgiving toward others?

_____

_____

_____

_____

_____

_____

_____

Scripture

Matthew 5:7: "Blessed are the merciful, for they will be shown mercy" (*Holy Bible NIV: New International Version*, n.d.).

Activity: Drawing

Draw a soft, gentle animal (like a lamb) and write about what gentleness means to you.

Day 6: Being Peacemakers

Scripture

Matthew 5:9: "Blessed are the peacemakers, for they will be called children of God" (*Holy Bible NIV: New International Version*, n.d.).

Affirmation

"I create peace in my relationships."

Activity: Role-Play

Role-play ways to handle conflict gently and peacefully.

Day 7: End-Of-Week Review

- **Recap:** Discuss and share what you've learned from this week's topic with your family.
- **Scripture:** Matthew 5:10: "Blessed are those who are persecuted because of righteousness" (*Holy Bible NIV: New International Version*, n.d.).

- **Family Activity:** Set aside one evening each week for a dedicated "Family Faith Night." Gather in your living room or backyard and start with a short devotional or Bible reading that focuses on being a strong believer. Afterward, engage in fun and meaningful activities such as creating a family vision board that illustrates your spiritual goals, writing encouraging notes to each other, or sharing personal stories of faith and how you've seen God work in your lives.
- **Preparation for Next Week:** The Bible is full of wonderful promises from God that remind us He is always with us, taking care of us and helping us through every situation. When we learn to trust God, we discover a sense of peace and confidence, knowing that He has a perfect plan for our lives. Let's explore how trusting in God can help us feel safe and loved, no matter what happens!

Week 34: Trust: Relying on God's Promises

Day 1: Confiding in God

Devotion

Trusting God means believing He will take care of us. We can lean on His promises because He loves us.

One chilly evening, a girl named Mia was worried about an upcoming school play. Although she had practiced her lines countless times, she still feared forgetting them in front of everyone. Remembering what her Sunday school teacher had taught her about trusting God, Mia closed her eyes and decided to pray.

"Dear God, I'm really scared. Please help me remember my lines and take away my fear," she whispered. As she finished her prayer, she felt a warm sense of peace wash over her. It was as if a weight had been lifted off her shoulders.

The next day at the play, Mia took a deep breath and stepped onto the stage. Instead of focusing on her fears, she chose to trust that God would help her. As she performed, she leaned on His promises, and much to her surprise, she delivered her lines with confidence. When the applause rang out at the end of the play, Mia smiled, realizing that trusting God had made all the difference. She learned that no matter what challenges she faced, she could always rely on God's love to take care of her.

Scripture

Proverbs 3:5-6: "Trust in the Lord with all your heart" (*Holy Bible NIV: New International Version*, n.d.).

Activity: Reflection

Write down one promise of God that brings you comfort. Reflect on it in your journal.

_____

_____

_____

_____

_____

_____

_____

Day 2: Trusting God's Plans

Scripture

Jeremiah 29:11: "For I know the plans I have for you" (*Holy Bible NIV: New International Version*, n.d.).

Affirmation

"God has a good plan for my life."

Activity: Art and Craft Project

Create a vision board representing your hopes and dreams for the future.

Day 3: God Is Truth

Discussion

God's promises are true, and He will never break them. How can we completely rely on His Words?

Scripture

Numbers 23:19: "God is not human, that he should lie" (*Holy Bible NIV: New International Version*, n.d.).

Activity: Challenge

Share with a friend or family member a promise from the Bible that you want to remember.

Day 4: Relying On God

Scripture

Philippians 4:6-7: "Do not be anxious about anything, but in every situation, by prayer and petition, present your requests to God" (*Holy Bible NIV: New International Version*, n.d.).

Prayer

Dear Lord,

Help me to remember to turn to You in prayer when I start to worry.

Remind me that I can bring all my thoughts to You. Teach me to trust in Your plans and find peace in Your presence.

Thank You for listening to me and for comforting me in times of need.

In Your Holy Name,

Amen.

Activity: Meditation

Practice breathing exercises to calm your mind while saying a simple prayer.

Day 5: Being Safe in God

God's love for us is always the same and never changes, no matter what happens. This means He loves us whether we're having a good day or a bad day. When we trust God, we can feel safe and secure, knowing that He is always with us to help and protect us. It's like having a cozy blanket that keeps us warm and safe! Trusting God helps us feel brave, even when things are scary or confusing. God's love is like a strong hug that we can hold on to at any time, giving us comfort and peace. We can always count on Him!

Journaling

Write a list of challenges you are facing. Next to each, write how God can help you through it.

_____

_____

_____

_____

_____

_____

_____

Scripture

Romans 8:38-39: "Nothing will separate us from the love of God" (*Holy Bible NIV: New International Version*, n.d.).

Activity: Art and Craft Project

Create a shield that represents God's protection, and write down ways you feel safe because of Him.

Day 6: Being Brave and Courageous

Scripture

Isaiah 41:10: "Do not fear, for I am with you; do not be dismayed, for I am your God" (*Holy Bible NIV: New International Version*, n.d.).

Affirmation

"I can be brave because God is with me."

Activity: Role-Play

Organize a role-playing session where kids can act out different scenarios that require courage. Prepare a list of situations, such as standing up for a friend being teased, trying something new (like a sport or art project), or speaking in front of a group. Have the kids take turns picking a scenario and acting it out, while the others can provide encouragement and suggestions for how to handle it courageously.

Day 7: End-Of-Week Review

- **Recap:** Discuss and share what you've learned from this week's topic with your family.
- **Scripture:** Psalm 147:11: "The Lord delights in those who fear him, who put their hope in his unfailing love" (*Holy Bible NIV: New International Version*, n.d.).
- **Family Activity:** Host a small celebration with friends or family to share what you are thankful for and how you trust God.
- **Preparation for Next Week:** Just like how every person has unique skills, such as being a great artist, a good listener, or a talented athlete, these gifts are meant to be shared and used for God's purposes. When we use our spiritual gifts, we not only bring joy to others but also grow closer to God and fulfill our unique role in His amazing plan. Let's explore how we can discover and use our talents to shine His light and spread love in our families, schools, and communities!

Week 35: Spiritual Gifts: Using Your Talents for God

Day 1: My Special Gifts

Devotion

God gives each of us special gifts and talents. We can use them to serve Him and others!

In the village of Nazareth, there lived a young boy named David who loved to play the harp. He spent countless hours in the fields, strumming beautiful melodies that echoed through the hills.

One day, a wise man named Samuel visited the village. He was searching for someone special, someone whom God had chosen to be the next king of Israel. As he walked through the village, he heard a lovely tune drifting through the air. Curious, he followed the sound until he found David playing his harp under a tree.

Samuel approached David and listened closely to his music. He saw not only the boy's talent but also the kindness in his heart and his love for God. Samuel realized that David had been given a special gift, one that could bring joy and comfort to others. After asking David to play a little more, he declared, "You have a wonderful gift, and God has big plans for you!"

As David continued to grow, he used his gift of music to serve his family and encourage his friends. David learned that his talent was not just for himself but a way to bring glory to God and help those around him.

Years later, when David became king, he never forgot how God had chosen him for a purpose. He continued to write songs of praise and lead the people in worship, showing everyone that each of us has special gifts and talents to share.

Scripture

1 Peter 4:10: "Each of you should use whatever gift you have received to serve others" (*Holy Bible NIV: New International Version*, n.d.).

Activity: Reflection

What are my spiritual gifts, and how can I use them to serve my family?

_____

_____

_____

_____

_____

_____

_____

Day 2: Growing My Gifts

Scripture

Romans 12:6-8: "We have different gifts, according to the grace given to each of us" (*Holy Bible NIV: New International Version*, n.d.).

Affirmation

"I discover and develop my gifts."

Activity: Challenge

Take a spiritual gifts quiz and discuss your results with someone.

Day 3: Using My Gifts for Church

Discussion

Discuss how using our gifts together creates a beautiful picture of God's work in our church and community.

Scripture

1 Corinthians 12:12: "For just as the body is one and has many members, so it is with Christ" (*Holy Bible NIV: New International Version*, n.d.).

Activity: Art and Craft Activity

Create a poster showing different gifts in the body of Christ, like serving, teaching, encouraging, etc.

Day 4: Sharing My Gifts to Help Others

Scripture

Ephesians 2:10: "For we are God's handiwork, created in Christ Jesus to do good works" (*Holy Bible NIV: New International Version*, n.d.).

Prayer

Dear Lord,

Thank You for the special gifts You have given me. Help me recognize these talents and how I can use them to bless others.

May my actions reflect Your love and bring happiness to those around me. Thank You for allowing me to serve You through my gifts.

In Jesus' Name,

Amen.

Activity: Challenge

Plan a small project where you can use your gifts to help someone (like cooking for a neighbor).

Day 5: Praising God for My Gifts

Each gift we have is unique and special, just like each of us! God made every person different on purpose, giving us our own talents and abilities. Some of us are great at drawing, while others are fantastic singers or amazing at solving puzzles. God loves us for who we are, and our unique gifts help us help others and make the world a better place. Embracing our differences is what makes life exciting and wonderful!

Reflection

Reflect on your talents and write them down. Share them with a friend or family member.

_____

_____

_____

_____

_____

_____

_____

Scripture

Psalm 139:14: "I praise you because I am fearfully and wonderfully made" (*Holy Bible NIV: New International Version*, n.d.).

Activity: Drawing

Draw a self-portrait and include symbols or words that represent your gifts.

Day 6: Developing My Gifts in God

Scripture

2 Timothy 1:6: "Fan into flame the gift of God" (*Holy Bible NIV: New International Version*, n.d.).

Affirmation

"I grow by using my spiritual gifts."

Activity: Journaling

Write in your journal about how you want to grow in your gifts this week.

Day 7: End-Of-Week Review

- **Recap:** Discuss and share what you've learned from this week's topic with your family.

- **Scripture:** Hebrews 10:24: "And let us consider how we may spur one another on toward love and good deeds" (*Holy Bible NIV: New International Version*, n.d.).

- **Family Activity:** Host an "open talent show" where everyone can share their gifts in a fun and supportive environment.

- **Preparation for Next Week:** The Golden Rule is a simple but powerful idea: treat others how you want to be treated!

Week 36: The Golden Rule: Treating Others the Way You Want to Be Treated

Day 1: What Is the Golden Rule?

Devotion

The Golden Rule teaches us to treat others kindly. If we want others to be nice to us, we should be nice to them, too!

In a cheerful little town, there was a boy named Alex who loved playing soccer. One day, while playing with his friends at the park, he noticed a new kid named Sam sitting all alone on a bench.

With a big smile, Alex ran over to Sam and said, "Hey! Want to join us for a game of soccer?" Sam looked surprised but excited, and he quickly nodded. As they played together, Alex made sure to pass the ball to Sam and encourage him with cheers whenever he kicked it. The two boys laughed and enjoyed the game, and soon, Sam became part of the group.

From that day on, Alex always remembered that kindness can go a long way and that treating others well is the key to building a supportive and joyful community!

Scripture

Matthew 7:12: "So in everything, do to others what you would have them do to you" (*Holy Bible NIV: New International Version*, n.d.).

Activity: Reflection

Reflect on a time someone was nice to you. Draw a picture of that moment.

_____

_____

_____

_____

_____

_____

_____

Day 2: Spreading Kindness

Scripture

Luke 6:31: "Do to others as you would have them do to you" (*Holy Bible NIV: New International Version*, n.d.).

Affirmation

"I spread joy through kindness."

Activity: Challenge

Write a small note to someone, thanking them for being kind or helpful.

Day 3: Practicing the Golden Rule

Discussion

Discuss why treating others well also means helping them when they are in need. We should be ready to lend a hand!

Scripture

James 2:1: "My brothers and sisters, believers in our glorious Lord Jesus Christ must not show favoritism" (*Holy Bible NIV: New International Version*, n.d.).

Activity: Challenge

Write down ways to express words of kindness to others.

_____

_____

_____

_____

_____

_____

_____

Day 4: Helping Others

Scripture

Galatians 6:2: "Carry each other's burdens" (*Holy Bible NIV: New International Version*, n.d.).

Prayer

Dear God,

Today, I ask for Your guidance to show me how I can help someone. Open my eyes to see those in need around me and fill my heart with compassion and kindness, so that I can make a positive difference in someone's day.

Thank You for the opportunity to be a helper.

In Jesus' Name,

Amen.

Activity: Challenge

Identify someone in need and plan a small way to assist them.

Day 5: Apologizing

Apologizing when we make mistakes is an important way to treat others kindly. When we accidentally hurt someone's feelings or do something wrong, saying sorry helps show that we care about them. Moreover, when we apologize, we take responsibility for our actions and let the other person know that we understand how they feel. As everyone makes mistakes, saying sorry is a brave step toward making things right and keeping our friendships strong!

Journaling

Apologizing when we make mistakes is also part of treating others well. How can I use prayers and God's Words to learn to accept and apologize to others?

_____

_____

_____

_____

_____

_____

_____

Scripture

Ephesians 4:32: "Be kind and compassionate to one another, forgiving each other" (*Holy Bible NIV: New International Version*, n.d.).

Activity: Art and Craft Activity

Design a poster that displays words of kindness and acceptance.

Day 6: Practicing Active Listening

Scripture

James 1:19: "Everyone should be quick to listen, slow to speak" (*Holy Bible NIV: New International Version*, n.d.).

Affirmation

"I listen carefully to others with love."

Activity: Challenge

Practice active listening with a friend by repeating what they said after they share.

Day 7: End-Of-Week Review

- **Recap:** Discuss and share what you've learned from this week's topic with your family.
- **Scripture:** 1 Peter 3:8: "Finally, all of you, be like-minded, be sympathetic, love one another" (*Holy Bible NIV: New International Version*, n.d.).

- **Family Activity:** Host a "kindness day" where everyone does one nice thing for someone else.
- **Preparation for Next Week:** When we express our gratitude, we not only make our hearts happier, but we also remind ourselves of God's goodness and love. Let's explore together how being thankful can brighten our days and help us see the world in a more joyful way!

Week 37: Thankfulness: Recognizing God's Gifts

Day 1: What Is Thankfulness?

Devotion

Thankfulness means recognizing all the wonderful things God has provided for us. We can be thankful daily!

A young shepherd named Eli looked after his sheep in a small village surrounded by gentle hills. Each day, he took them to green fields and clear streams, finding joy in the beauty of nature, even when he felt lonely. One evening, as the sun set, Eli sat on a grassy hill, watching his sheep munch away. He thought about how God took care of him not just with sheep but also with stunning views, soft winds, and twinkling stars.

Remembering the Psalmist's words, "The Lord is my shepherd, I will not need," Eli felt a warm feeling of thankfulness. The next morning, Eli wanted to show his gratitude. He picked fresh bread and fruit from his garden and went to visit his neighbors. He knocked on Naomi's door, a kind widow who always seemed tired. When she saw Eli and his gift, her face brightened. "Eli, what a lovely surprise!" she said. "But why did you bring this to me?" "I'm thankful for everything God gives us each day, and I wanted to share my blessings with you," Eli explained. "We often think about what we don't have, but every little thing—from sunshine to friendship—deserves appreciation."

Soon, news of Eli's kindness spread through the village, and many villagers began sharing their blessings too. Every day turned into a thankful celebration, where neighbors came together to enjoy food, share stories, and laugh, recognizing all the beautiful gifts God had given them.

Scripture

1 Thessalonians 5:18: "Give thanks in all circumstances" (*Holy Bible NIV: New International Version*, n.d.).

Activity: Reflection

Write down five things you are thankful for today.

1. _____

2. _____
3. _____
4. _____
5. _____

Day 2: The Goodness of God

Scripture

Psalm 107:1: "Give thanks to the Lord, for he is good" (*Holy Bible NIV: New International Version*, n.d.).

Affirmation

"I recognize the goodness of God in my life."

Activity: Prayer

Create a prayer thanking God for all the good things you receive in your life.

Day 3: Filling My Heart With Joy

Discussion

Discuss how thankfulness can change our hearts! When we are grateful, we feel happier and more content.

Scripture

Colossians 3:15: "And be thankful" (*Holy Bible NIV: New International Version*, n.d.).

Activity: Challenge

Notice three things today that make you happy. Share them with a friend or family member.

Day 4: Being Grateful for Others

Scripture

Philippians 1:3: "I thank my God every time I remember you" (*Holy Bible NIV: New International Version*, n.d.).

Prayer

Dear God,

Thank You for the special people in my life. Thank You for my family who loves me and cares for me. Thank You for my friends who bring joy and fun to my days.

I am grateful for the moments we share; may we always appreciate each other and grow together.

Thank You for all the love around me, God! I am truly blessed.

In Jesus' Name,

Amen.

Activity: Challenge

Write a letter expressing your gratitude to someone special in your life.

_____

_____

_____

_____

Day 5: Building Stronger Bonds

When we say thank you and show gratitude for what others do for us, like when a friend shares their toys or helps us with homework, it makes them feel appreciated and loved. This tiny act can brighten their day and encourage them to do nice things for us again. When we express gratitude, we create closer connections and trust with others. The more we practice thankfulness, the happier and stronger our friendships will be.

Reflection

Thankfulness can help strengthen our relationships. How can I express gratitude through my words and actions?

_____

_____

_____

_____

_____

_____

_____

Scripture

Proverbs 18:24: "A man who has friends must himself be friendly" (*Holy Bible NIV: New International Version*, n.d.).

Activity: Art and Craft Activity

Create a "Thankfulness Tree" by drawing a tree and writing things you're thankful for on its leaves.

Day 6: Faith and Thankfulness

Scripture

Psalm 136:1: "Give thanks to the Lord for he is good" (*Holy Bible NIV: New International Version.*, n.d.).

Affirmation

"My thankfulness strengthens my faith."

Activity: Challenge

Share with a friend or family member a moment when you felt thankful and how it affected your faith.

Day 7: End-Of-Week Review

- **Recap:** Discuss and share what you've learned from this week's topic with your family.
- **Scripture:** 2 Corinthians 9:15: "Thanks be to God for his indescribable gift." (*Holy Bible NIV: New International Version*, n.d.).
- **Family Activity:** Create a gratitude collage using pictures, drawings, or words that represent what you're thankful for.

- **Preparation for Next Week:** Imagine walking through a dark tunnel where everything feels a bit scary and uncertain. Now, think about a bright light shining at the end of that tunnel, guiding you safely to the other side. That's what being a beacon of hope means! Just like that light, we can spread kindness, love, and encouragement to those around us, especially during tough times. When we share our smiles and help others, we become a shining light in their lives, reminding them that no matter how dark things may seem, there is always hope and warmth waiting to be found. Together, we can brighten the world!

Week 38: Light in the Darkness: Being a Beacon of Hope

Day 1: Shining God's Love

Devotion

Just as a light guides us in the dark, we can bring hope to others by shining God's love.

A girl named Sarah lived in a small village surrounded by tall mountains. The villagers often spoke of an ancient story that told of a powerful light hidden within the hills, a light that could guide lost travelers and bring hope to those in despair. Inspired by the story, Sarah dreamed of finding this light to help her friends and neighbors.

One evening, Sarah gathered her courage and set off toward the mountains. With each step, she recalled the words from the Bible: "You are the light of the world. A city set on a hill cannot be hidden."

As she climbed, she encountered a weary traveler named Matthew, who had lost his way. Seeing his despair, Sarah approached him and offered her hand. "Don't worry, I'll help you find your way. God's love shines brightly in our hearts, and together, we can find the path."

Together, they continued their journey, sharing stories of faith and joy. Sarah's words sparked hope in Matthew, and he began to feel the fear fade as they moved closer to the mountain peak. Finally, after what felt like an adventure, they reached a clearing where the moonlight spilled like silver over the landscape.

At that moment, they spotted a beautiful lantern hanging from a tree, glowing brightly. The lantern's light illuminated the path back to the village. Sarah smiled, realizing that this was the light spoken of in the ancient story, and it was their love and friendship that had led them there.

They returned to the village together, carrying the lantern and sharing the light with others. The villagers gathered around, inspired by their journey and the light they had found.

Scripture

Matthew 5:16: "Let your light shine before others" (*Holy Bible NIV: New International Version*, n.d.).

Activity: Drawing

Draw a picture of a light shining in the darkness and write about how you can be that light.

_____

_____

_____

_____

_____

_____

_____

Day 2: Bringing Hope

Scripture

Isaiah 42:6: "I will keep you and will make you to be a covenant for the people" (*Holy Bible NIV: New International Version*, n.d.).

Affirmation

"I bring hope to those in need."

Activity: Challenge

Think of someone who needs hope and plan a way to encourage them.

Day 3: Following the Light of Jesus

Discussion

Jesus is our ultimate light. Discuss how we can find guidance and strength in dark times through His love.

Scripture

John 8:12: "I am the light of the world" (*Holy Bible NIV: New International Version*, n.d.).

Activity: Reflection

Write down how Jesus has brought light to your life.

_____

_____

_____

_____

_____

_____

_____

Day 4: Being Chosen by God

Scripture

1 Peter 2:9: "You are a chosen people, a royal priesthood" (*Holy Bible NIV: New International Version*, n.d.).

Prayer

Dear God,

Thank You for loving me with a love that is pure and endless. Help me to be a reflection of Your love in all that I do.

Teach me to show compassion to those who are hurting and to lend a helping hand to those in need.

Remind me each day that I am a part of Your family and that through me, Your love can touch the hearts of many.

I am grateful for the opportunity to reflect Your heart to the world!

In Jesus' Name,

Amen.

Activity: Challenge

Create a "Hope Jar" filled with encouraging notes. Share them with friends.

Day 5: Being a Light

Helping others in need is like bringing a bright light into a dark room! When we do kind things for someone, like sharing a snack, helping them with their homework, or simply listening to them, we make their day a little brighter. These kind actions can lift their spirits and show them they are not alone. Even small acts of kindness, like a smile or a compliment, can spread joy and hope and light up the darkness around us.

Reflection

Reflect on a time you faced a challenge and found strength through God. Write about it.

_____

_____

_____

_____

_____

_____

_____

Scripture

Ephesians 5:8: "For you were once darkness, but now you are light in the Lord" (*Holy Bible NIV: New International Version*, n.d.).

Activity: Drawing

Draw a picture of a light shining in the darkness and write about how you can be that light.

Day 6: Carrying God's Light

Scripture

2 Corinthians 4:6: "For God, who said, 'Let light shine out of darkness,' made his light shine in our hearts" (*Holy Bible NIV: New International Version*, n.d.).

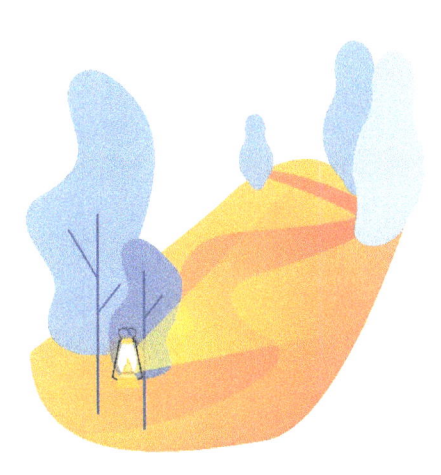

Affirmation

"I am strong because I carry God's light."

Activity: Challenge

Plan a small service project where you can demonstrate kindness and generosity.

Day 7: End-Of- Week Review

- **Recap:** Discuss and share what you've learned from this week's topic with your family.
- **Scripture:** Philippians 2:15: "You shine like stars in the sky" (*Holy Bible NIV: New International Version*, n.d.).
- **Family Activity:** Plan a "light-themed" gathering with friends or family, where everyone shares how they can shine God's light.
- **Preparation for Next Week:** Have you ever faced something really tough, like learning to ride a bike or finishing a big puzzle? Endurance is all about staying strong and not giving up, even when things get challenging! When problems come our way, whether it's a difficult homework assignment or a disagreement with a friend, having endurance helps us keep trying and believing in ourselves. With God's help, we can face any trial, knowing that every challenge we overcome makes us stronger and braver!

Week 39: Endurance: Staying Strong in Trials

Day 1: What Is Endurance?

Devotion

Endurance means staying strong even when things are tough. God is with us through every challenge we face!

In the bustling town of Jericho, there lived a determined young boy named David. He loved to play outside, climb trees, and explore the world around him. One day, while exploring the valley beyond his home, David came across a steep mountain that towered over the landscape. He gazed at the summit and felt a desire to reach the top. "I can do this!" he declared, filled with excitement and courage.

The next morning, he set out early, ready to embrace the challenge. As he began his climb, the path grew rocky and steep. Halfway up, dark clouds gathered, and rain began to pour. David stumbled, feeling scared and unsure. It would be so easy to turn back, but then he remembered the words of Scripture he had learned from his grandparents: "I can do all things through Christ who strengthens me." With a deep breath, he pressed on, determined not to let the rain stop him.

As he continued to climb, he encountered obstacles—slippery rocks, thick bushes, and steep cliffs. Each time he faced a challenge, he whispered a prayer, asking God for strength and guidance. "God, help me stay strong, even when it's tough," he prayed. And through each difficulty, David felt a warm sensation in his heart, reminding him that God was right there with him, cheering him on.

Finally, after hours of climbing, David reached the summit. He stood on top of the mountain, breathless and filled with joy. The view was breathtaking—a beautiful landscape stretching as far as he could see.

He shouted with excitement, thanking God for the endurance that had helped him succeed.

Scripture

James 1:2-3: "Consider it pure joy, my brothers and sisters, whenever you face trials of many kinds" (*Holy Bible NIV: New International Version*, n.d.).

Activity: Journaling

Journal about a time when you faced a challenge and how you overcame it.

_____

_____

_____

_____

_____

_____

_____

Day 2: Growing Stronger Through Challenges

Scripture

Romans 5:3-4: "Suffering produces perseverance; perseverance, character; and character, hope" (*Holy Bible NIV: New International Version*, n.d.).

Affirmation

"I grow stronger through my challenges."

Activity: Challenge

Create a "Growth Chart" showing how you have grown through difficult experiences.

Day 3: Trusting God

Discussion

Discuss why relying on God during trials brings comfort and strength as we can pray for help and support.

Scripture

Philippians 4:13: "I can do all this through him who gives me strength" (*Holy Bible NIV: New International Version*, n.d.).

Activity: Prayer

Write a prayer requesting strength for any current challenges you are facing.

_____

_____

_____

_____

_____

_____

_____

Day 4: Thanking God for Your Victories

Scripture

Ecclesiastes 4:9-10: "Two are better than one... If either of them falls down, one can help the other up" (*Holy Bible NIV: New International Version*, n.d.).

Prayer

Dear God,

Thank You for always being there for me in times of joy and in times of trouble. Help me to remember that it's okay to ask for help and that I don't have to face challenges alone.

Help me to be open and honest about how I feel and remind me that seeking help is a sign of strength.

Thank You for the gift of friendship and love. Help me to lean on others when I need help, God!

In Your Holy Name,

Amen.

Activity: Challenge

Write down your victories over challenges, and thank God for helping you through them.

_____

_____

_____

_____

_____

_____

Day 5: God's Promises

Going through tough times or trials can be challenging, but they help us learn to trust God even more. When things are hard, we might feel sad or worried, but this is a chance to remember that God has promised to take care of us. Just like a superhero always stands by us, God is always faithful and will help us through our struggles. Enduring through these hard times helps us grow stronger and believe that God is with us no matter what.

Reflection

Reflect on one of God's promises. Share it with someone and discuss its importance.

_____

_____

_____

_____

_____

_____

Scripture

Lamentations 3:22-23: "His mercies are new every morning" (*Holy Bible NIV: New International Version*, n.d.).

Activity: Drawing

Draw a vibrant rainbow arching across a peaceful landscape. Below the rainbow, you can illustrate a scene that represents various promises from the Bible.

Day 6: Finding Rest in God

Scripture

Matthew 11:28: "Come to me, all you who are weary and burdened, and I will give you rest" (*Holy Bible NIV: New International Version*, n.d.).

Affirmation

"I find rest in God during hard times."

Activity: Challenge

Create a "Comfort Corner" at home where you can go when you need help or rest.

Day 7: End-Of-Week Review

- **Recap:** Discuss and share what you've learned from this week's topic with your family.
- **Scripture:** 2 Timothy 4:7: "I have fought the good fight, I have finished the race" (*Holy Bible NIV: New International Version*, n.d.).
- **Activity:** Gather with your family members and talk about a challenge you are facing and ask for support.
- **Preparation for Next Week:** Have you ever given up something special to help someone else or to make your friend happy? That's what sacrifice is all about! It means putting others first and giving your best, even if it costs you something you love. Just like how we see in stories where characters choose to help their friends or family, we can learn that true kindness often involves making sacrifices. When we share our toys, time, or talents, we show love and care for those around us. Understanding sacrifice helps us appreciate the importance of giving and reminds us that the best gifts come from the heart!

Week 40: Sacrifice: Understanding Giving Your Best

Day 1: What Is Sacrifice?

Devotion

Sacrifice means giving up something we value to help or support others. Jesus showed us the ultimate sacrifice by giving His life for us.

A compassionate woman named Ruth lived in a small village nestled between hills. Known for her warm smile, she dedicated her life to caring for the sick and needy.

Ruth had a daughter named Sarah, who was her pride and joy. One bitterly cold night, Ruth received word that a family down the road desperately needed help. They were running low on food and were too ill to care for themselves.

Although she was worried about Sarah, Ruth decided to act. She gathered what little food they had and set out into the night, knowing she might not have enough left for herself and her daughter.

Upon reaching the family's door, Ruth knocked and was greeted with tired eyes. She offered them not only the food she had but also her time and care. She stayed through the night, nursing them back to health and comforting them with her presence.

She understood that true sacrifice meant giving up something valuable for the sake of love and compassion.

Scripture

John 15:13: "Greater love has no one than this: to lay down one's life for one's friends" (*Holy Bible NIV: New International Version*, n.d.).

Activity: Reflection

Reflect on someone who has sacrificed for you and write them a thank-you note.

Day 2: Making Sacrifices

Reflection

Reflect on how sometimes sacrificing means giving our time or talents to help others. It's a way to serve as Jesus did.

Scripture

Mark 10:45: "For even the Son of Man did not come to be served, but to serve" (*Holy Bible NIV: New International Version*, n.d.).

Activity: Challenge

Volunteer your time to help someone or a cause in your community.

Day 3: Worshipping God Through Sacrifices

Discussion

Discuss why when we give our best to God and others, it's a form of worship. Sacrificing from our hearts shows our love.

Scripture

Romans 12:1: "Present your bodies as a living sacrifice, holy and acceptable to God" (*Holy Bible NIV: New International Version*, n.d.).

Activity: Challenge

Write a list of what "giving my best" means to you. Share it with a friend.

_____

_____

_____

_____

_____

_____

_____

Day 4: Being Humble

Scripture

Philippians 2:3: "In humility value others above yourselves" (*Holy Bible NIV: New International Version*, n.d.).

Prayer

Dear God,

Help me to embrace humility in my heart. Teach me to see the value in serving others, to recognize their needs before my own, and to approach each interaction with kindness and compassion.

When I am faced with opportunities to help, give me the courage to act selflessly and generously.

Fill me with Your Spirit, so that my actions reflect Your grace and mercy.

Thank You for the reminder that every act of service, no matter how small, has the power to make a difference.

In Your holy name, I pray,

Amen.

Activity: Challenge

Plan a small act of kindness for someone in need this week.

Day 5: True Love

Sacrifice means giving up something we want or like to help others, and it's not always easy. For example, sharing your favorite toy or helping a friend instead of playing by yourself shows you care. When we make sacrifices, it shows true love and commitment to our friends and family. We can encourage each other to be selfless by cheering each other on and reminding one another of the joy that comes from caring for others.

Reflection

How can I show true love and sacrifice for others?

_____

_____

_____

_____

_____

_____

_____

Scripture

Ephesians 5:2: "Walk in the way of love, just as Christ loved us and gave himself up for us" (*Holy Bible NIV: New International Version*, n.d.).

Activity: Drawing

Illustrate a large heart intertwined with a cross, symbolizing Jesus' ultimate sacrifice for love. Surround it with blooming flowers to signify growth and beauty that comes from true love.

Day 6: God Provides All I Need

Scripture

Philippians 4:19: "And my God will meet all your needs according to the riches of his glory in Christ Jesus" (*Holy Bible NIV: New International Version*, n.d.).

Affirmation

"I trust God to provide for me."

Activity: Journaling

Create a "sacrifice and provision" journal. Write down sacrifices you make and how God provides for you.

Day 7: End-Of-Week Review

- **Recap:** Discuss and share what you've learned from this week's topic with your family.
- **Scripture:** Luke 6:38: "Give, and it will be given to you" (*Holy Bible NIV: New International Version*, n.d.).
- **Family Activity:** Host a gratitude celebration where everyone shares their experiences related to sacrifices and blessings.
- **Preparation for Next Week:** Have you ever wondered what happens after we leave this world? In our journey of faith, we learn about something amazing called eternity—the promise of Heaven! It's a special place where we can live forever with God, filled with love, joy, and peace. Imagine exploring beautiful gardens, meeting friendly angels, and being with all the people we love! Eternity means that even though life on Earth can be tough sometimes, we have a wonderful future to look forward to where happiness never ends.

Week 41: Eternity: The Promise of Heaven

Day 1: The Gift of Heaven

Devotion

Heaven is a special place where God lives and where we will be with Him forever.

Once upon a time, in a small village, there was a curious boy named Daniel. One evening, as the stars twinkled brightly in the night sky, Daniel sat at his grandmother's feet, eager to hear more.

"Tell me, Grandma," he said, "what is Heaven like?"

His grandmother smiled gently and began to weave a tale. "Heaven, my dear, is a special place where God lives. Imagine the most beautiful garden you've ever seen. In this garden, there are no worries, no pain, and everyone is filled with joy."

Daniel's eyes sparkled with excitement. "But who will be there?"

"With God's love surrounding us," she continued, "we will be with our loved ones, our friends, and even the angels who sing songs of praise."

"But how do we reach this special place?" Daniel asked, filled with hope.

"You see, my child," his grandmother replied, "there are many paths in life, but the way to Heaven is through faith in God and by loving others as He loves us. When we show kindness, help those in need, and believe in God's promises, we are walking the road to Heaven."

As Daniel listened, his heart swelled with comfort and joy. He imagined the heavenly garden, where he could run freely and play with his loved ones forever. That night, he closed his eyes, dreaming of the day he would be with God in Heaven, filled with love and happiness.

Scripture

John 14:2-3: "In my Father's house are many mansions: if it were not so, I would have told you. I go to prepare a place for you. And if I go and prepare a place for you, I will come again, and receive you unto myself; that where I am, there ye may be also" (*Holy Bible NIV: New International Version*, n.d.).

Activity: Drawing

Draw a picture of what you think Heaven looks like.

Day 2: Our Hope in Heaven

Scripture

Romans 15:13: "Now the God of hope fill you with all joy and peace in believing, that ye may abound in hope, through the power of the Holy Ghost" (*Holy Bible NIV: New International Version*, n.d.).

Affirmation

"I have hope because of the promise of Heaven."

Activity: Reflection

Reflect on what makes you hopeful and write it in your journal.

_____
_____
_____
_____
_____
_____
_____

Day 3: Living for Eternity

Discussion

Discuss how we can choose to do good things now that will matter forever.

Scripture

Matthew 6:20: "But lay up for yourselves treasures in heaven, where neither moth nor rust doth corrupt, and where thieves do not break through nor steal" (*Holy Bible NIV: New International Version*, n.d.).

Activity: Challenge

Create a service project to help someone in need.

Day 4: Celebrating God's Promise

Scripture

John 3:16: "For God so loved the world, that he gave his only begotten Son, that whosoever believeth in him should not perish, but have everlasting life" (*Holy Bible NIV: New International Version*, n.d.).

Prayer

Dear Jesus,

Thank You for the amazing gift of eternal life, where I can be with You forever. Help me to remember how special this gift is and to share Your love with others.

Please fill my heart with joy and kindness, and help me to be a good friend, just like You are. When I feel scared or lonely, remind me that You are always with me, and I have a wonderful future ahead.

Thank You for being my Savior and for always watching over me. I love You, Jesus!

Amen.

Activity: Challenge

Play a faith-based game with your friends that teaches about God's love.

Day 5: Faith Journey

Our journey of faith is like an exciting adventure that brings us closer to the wonderful promise of Heaven! When we believe in God and follow His teachings, we learn more about His love and kindness. Each step we take in our faith, like praying, helping others, and being kind, helps us grow and understand God better. Heaven is a special place where we will be with God forever, free from sadness. As we follow our journey of faith, we can look forward to this amazing promise and share God's love with others along the way!

Activity: Challenge

Go on a nature walk, reflecting on God's creation and your faith journey, and write down your thoughts.

_____

_____

_____

_____

_____

_____

_____

Scripture

Hebrews 11:1: "Now faith is the substance of things hoped for, the evidence of things not seen" (*Holy Bible NIV: New International Version*, n.d.).

Activity: Drawing

Draw a winding path that leads from a dark, hilly area to a bright, beautiful landscape with gates made of pearl. Along the path, illustrate footprints representing faith, with small icons like hearts and stars to symbolize hope and love leading the way.

Day 6: Sharing the Good News

Scripture

Mark 16:15: "And he said unto them, Go ye into all the world, and preach the gospel to every creature" (*Holy Bible NIV: New International Version*, n.d.).

Affirmation

"I will share the good news of Jesus with others."

Activity: Art and Craft Activity

Make a drawing or craft that shows what Heaven means to you and share it.

Day 7: End-Of-Week Review

- **Recap:** Discuss and share what you've learned from this week's topic with your family.
- **Scripture:** 1 Thessalonians 5:18: "In everything give thanks: for this is the will of God in Christ Jesus concerning you" (*Holy Bible NIV: New International Version*, n.d.).
- **Family Activity:** Gather for a family prayer, thanking God for all the blessings and expressing hope for the promise of Heaven.
- **Preparation for Next Week:** Sometimes, we might feel shy or scared about talking to others about what we believe, but being bold means we can share our love for God without fear. Just like superheroes who stand up for what's right, we can tell our friends about the amazing things God has done in our lives. Let's learn how to be bold together and spread the good news of God's love!

Week 42: Boldness: Sharing Your Faith Without Fear

Day 1: Being Brave for Jesus

Devotion

God wants us to be brave and share our faith without being afraid.

In a little town, there lived a young girl named Mia. One day, her teacher announced that they would have a "Show and Tell" day, where everyone could speak about something they believed in.

Mia's heart raced. She considered talking about her favorite book or her pet, but deep inside, she felt a gentle tug to share about her faith in God. She remembered the stories of the brave disciples from the Bible who traveled far and wide to spread the message of Jesus, even when it was scary.

That night, Mia prayed for courage and guidance. The next day, standing in front of her classmates, she took a deep breath and began to share how much God loved her and how He was always there for her, especially in tough times. To her surprise, her friends listened intently, and some even asked questions!

After her presentation, several classmates thanked Mia for her words and admitted they had been curious about faith but didn't know how to start. Encouraged by their responses, Mia realized that sharing her faith was not only brave but also brought people together.

Scripture

2 Timothy 1:7: "For God did not give us a spirit of timidity, but a spirit of power, of love and of self-discipline" (*Holy Bible NIV: New International Version*, n.d.).

Activity: Challenge

Practice saying your faith story to a family member.

Day 2: Trusting God's Strength

Scripture

Isaiah 41:10: "Fear thou not; for I am with thee: be not dismayed; for I am thy God: I will strengthen thee; yea, I will help thee; yea, I will uphold thee with the right hand of my righteousness" (*Holy Bible NIV: New International Version*, n.d.).

Affirmation

"God gives me strength to be brave."

Activity: Challenge

List situations where you need to be bold and pray about them.

___

___

___

___

___

___

___

Day 3: Sharing With Friends

Discussion

Discuss why it's important to share Jesus with our friends.

Scripture

Matthew 5:14: "Ye are the light of the world. A city that is set on a hill cannot be hid" (*Holy Bible NIV: New International Version*, n.d.).

Activity: Drawing

Create a bright poster about sharing Jesus and hang it in your room.

Day 4: Speaking Up for What Is Right

Scripture

Proverbs 31:8: "Open thy mouth for the dumb in the cause of all such as are appointed to destruction" (*Holy Bible NIV: New International Version*, n.d.).

Prayer

Dear Lord,

Help me to stand up for You in every situation I face. When I feel afraid or unsure, remind me that You are always by my side, guiding me with Your love.

Teach me to speak up when I see injustice and to defend those who cannot defend themselves.

Lord, I trust in Your power and grace to help me live boldly for You each day.

Thank You for listening to my heart. I love You, Lord!

Amen.

Activity: Role-Play

Role-play different scenarios where you can speak up kindly.

Day 5: Sharing the Good News

Sharing the good news of Jesus is super important because it's all about spreading love and hope! When we tell others about Jesus, we share how much He loves us and how He can make our lives better. Jesus teaches us to be kind, forgive others, and care for one another. By sharing His story, we can help our friends and family understand how special He is and how they can be part of God's family, too.

Reflection

How can I share the good news each day?

_____

_____

_____

_____

_____

_____

_____

Scripture

Romans 10:15: "And how shall they preach, except they be sent? (*Holy Bible NIV: New International Version*, n.d.).

Activity: Drawing

Illustrate a colorful bird carrying a scroll in its beak, flying over a cheerful landscape. The scroll can have the words "Good News" written on it, symbolizing the spreading of God's message of love and hope.

Day 6: Overcoming Fear

Scripture

Psalm 56:3: "What time I am afraid, I will trust in thee" (*Holy Bible NIV: New International Version*, n.d.).

Affirmation

"I will not be afraid because God is with me."

Activity: Challenge

Create a "Fear Jar" and write down your fears to pray over them.

Day 7: Celebrating Boldness

- **Recap:** Discuss and share what you've learned from this week's topic with your family.
- **Scripture:** Acts 4:29: "And now, Lord, behold their threatenings: and grant unto thy servants, that with all boldness they may speak thy word." (*Holy Bible NIV: New International Version.*, n.d.)
- **Family Activity:** Gather with your family members and take turns sharing a fun story or experience where you were able to be bold in your faith.
- **Preparation for Next Week:** Did you know that the words we use have amazing power? They can make people feel happy, loved, and encouraged, or they can hurt their feelings and bring them down. That's why it's important to think about what we say! When we speak life and truth, we're spreading kindness and positivity, just like superheroes spreading good vibes! Our words can brighten someone's day or help a friend who is feeling sad. Let's learn how to use our words to uplift others and share God's love through the powerful things we say!

Week 43: The Power of Words: Speaking Life and Truth

Day 1: Words Matter

Devotion

Our words have the power to build others up or tear them down.

In a quaint village, there lived a young girl named Clara. Clara was known for her bright smile and cheerful spirit, but she often struggled with finding the right words to say. One day, while playing with her friends, she overheard two of them, Lily and Ben, whispering about a new girl named Mary who had just moved to the village.

"Did you see those shoes Mary wore? They are so old-fashioned! I bet no one will want to be friends with her," Lily laughed.

Clara felt a knot in her stomach. She knew words could hurt, and she remembered a story her grandmother told her from the Bible about the power of words. The story of how King Solomon, known for his wisdom, taught that "the tongue has the power of life and death."

Taking a deep breath, Clara approached her friends. "Maybe Mary's shoes are different, but we don't know her story," she said. "What if those shoes mean something special to her? Let's not make fun of her. Instead, why don't we invite her to play with us?"

Gathering her courage, Clara walked over to Mary, who was sitting alone on a bench, looking lost. "Hi there! I'm Clara. Do you want to join us for a game?" Clara asked with a warm smile.

Mary's eyes brightened, and she said, "Really? I'd love to!"

As the day went on, Clara took the opportunity to get to know Mary. She discovered that Mary loved to draw and had just moved to the village from far away. Clara encouraged her, saying, "Your drawings are amazing! I'd love to see more of them!" Mary beamed with pride.

Later, when Clara sat down with her friends, she said, "You know, our words can either build someone up or tear them down. I'm glad we welcomed Mary instead of making fun of her."

Lily nodded thoughtfully. "You're right, Clara. I'm sorry for what I said earlier. From now on, I want to use my words to be kind and lift others up, just like you did."

In that moment, Clara learned that standing up for others and using kind words could change a person's day for the better. As they all played together, Clara felt pride in her heart, knowing she had chosen to use her words to build a new friendship rather than tear someone down.

Scripture

Proverbs 18:21: "Death and life are in the power of the tongue: and they that love it shall eat the fruit thereof" (*Holy Bible NIV: New International Version*, n.d.).

Activity: Challenge

Write a note of encouragement to someone and give it to them.

Day 2: Kind Words

Journaling

Make a list of 10 kind words that can make a big difference in someone's day.

1. _____
2. _____
3. _____
4. _____
5. _____
6. _____
7. _____
8. _____
9. _____

10. _____

Scripture

Ephesians 4:32: "And be ye kind one to another, tenderhearted, forgiving one another, even as God for Christ's sake hath forgiven you" (*Holy Bible NIV: New International Version*, n.d.).

Affirmation

"I will speak kindness to everyone I meet."

Activity: Challenge

Create a kindness calendar for the week with positive things to say each day.

Day 3: Truth in Our Words

Discussion

Discuss why we should always speak the truth, just like Jesus.

Scripture

John 8:32: "And ye shall know the truth, and the truth shall make you free" (*Holy Bible NIV: New International Version*, n.d.).

Activity: Drawing

Draw a picture that shows the importance of honesty.

Day 4: Words of Wisdom

Scripture

Proverbs 1:5: "A wise man will hear, and will increase learning; and a man of understanding shall attain unto wise counsels" (*Holy Bible NIV: New International Version*, n.d.).

Prayer

Dear Lord,

In all my decisions, both big and small, please grant me the clarity to choose what aligns with Your will. Help me to listen to Your voice and trust the direction You lead me in.

Thank You for being a constant source of wisdom and strength. I trust in Your plans for me and believe that with Your help, I can grow in understanding and make decisions that bring glory to Your name.

Amen.

Activity: Journaling

Write down a wise saying or proverb you like in your journal.

Day 5: Praying With Our Words

Prayer is a special way to connect with God, just like talking to a friend. When we pray, we can tell God what's on our hearts, like our hopes, worries, or things we're thankful for. We can ask for help or guidance, and we can also say thank you for all the good things in our lives. There's no right or wrong way to pray; it can be as simple as speaking with a friend.

Journaling

Write down prayers about your day and what's on your heart.

_____

_____

_____

_____

_____

_____

Scripture

Philippians 4:6: "Be careful for nothing; but in every thing by prayer and supplication with thanksgiving let your requests be made known unto God" (*Holy Bible NIV: New International Version*, n.d.).

Activity: Drawing

Illustrate a pair of hands clasped together in prayer, surrounded by glowing light or sparkles. Above the hands, depict thought bubbles with various symbols representing different prayers, such as a heart for love, a cross for faith, and a globe for peace.

Day 6: Words that Bless

Scripture

Numbers 6:24-26: "The Lord bless thee, and keep thee: The Lord make his face shine upon thee, and be gracious unto thee: The Lord lift up his countenance upon thee, and give thee peace" (*Holy Bible NIV: New International Version*, n.d.).

Affirmation

"I speak blessings over my friends and family!"

Activity: Challenge

Write a blessing for each family member and share it.

Day 7: Reflecting on Our Words

- **Recap:** Discuss and share what you've learned from this week's topic with your family.
- **Scripture:** James 1:19: "Wherefore, my beloved brethren, let every man be swift to hear, slow to speak, slow to wrath" (*Holy Bible NIV: New International Version*, n.d.).
- **Family Activity:** Gather as a family and create scenarios where words can have different effects (both positive and negative). For example, one person can pretend to be a friend who is feeling down while another uses kind words to uplift them. Discuss how different words made everyone feel and the importance of choosing our words wisely.
- **Preparation for Next Week:** Just like superheroes who stand up for what's right, we can show righteousness in our everyday lives by being honest, kind, and helping others. Let's explore how we can choose to do what is right and make the world a better place together!

Week 44: Righteousness: Choosing to Do What is Right

Day 1: What Is Righteousness?

Devotion

Righteousness means doing what is right in God's eyes.

Once, in a small village nestled between lush mountains, there lived a humble farmer named Elias. Known for his unwavering faith, he devoted his life to his crops and his family. He believed deeply in the concept of righteousness—doing what is right in God's eyes.

One morning, as he toiled in his fields, a stranger arrived, weary and hungry. Elias took the man in, offering him food and shelter for the night. The stranger, grateful for the kindness, revealed that he was a traveler on a quest to find a legendary treasure hidden deep in the mountains. Many had sought it, but none had returned.

Intrigued, Elias felt a pull towards this adventure, believing that perhaps the treasure could help his village thrive. Yet, as dusk fell, he consulted his heart and prayed for guidance. He felt a gentle whisper within: "True wealth lies not in gold, but in righteousness."

That night, Elias made his decision. He would not seek the treasure for himself but instead use his humble means to help others. The next morning, he shared his food with other villagers, urging them to plant more crops and support one another. Inspired by his selflessness, many joined him in his mission.

Days turned into weeks, and while the treasure remained elusive, the village began to flourish. People worked together, sharing resources and joy. They celebrated harvests with feasts, laughter, and gratitude. Elias realized that by prioritizing righteousness over riches, he had uncovered a far greater treasure—the love and unity of his community.

Years later, when the traveler returned, he found the village transformed. He asked Elias about the treasure. Smiling, Elias replied, "It was never hidden in gold but found in the hearts of those who choose to do what is right in God's eyes."

Scripture

Matthew 5:6: "Blessed are they which do hunger and thirst after righteousness: for they shall be filled" (*Holy Bible NIV: New International Version*, n.d.).

Activity: Reflection

Write down what righteousness means to you.

_____

_____

_____

_____

_____

_____

_____

Day 2: Standing Up for What Is Right

Scripture

Isaiah 1:17: "Learn to do well; seek judgment, relieve the oppressed, judge the fatherless, plead for the widow" (*Holy Bible NIV: New International Version*, n.d.).

Affirmation

"I will stand up for justice."

Activity: Role-Play

Role-play a scenario where you need to stand up for a friend.

Day 3: Making Good Choices

Discussion

Discuss the importance of good decisions with a family member.

Scripture

Proverbs 3:5-6: "Trust in the Lord with all your heart and lean not on your own understanding; in all your ways acknowledge Him, and He will make your paths straight" (*Holy Bible NIV: New International Version*, n.d.).

Activity: Reflection

Think of how we can make choices every day that please God.

_____

_____

_____

_____

_____

_____

_____

Day 3: Standing Up for What Is Right

Scripture

Isaiah 1:17: "Learn to do right; seek justice. Defend the oppressed. Take up the cause of the fatherless; plead the case of the widow" (*Holy Bible NIV: New International Version*, n.d.).

Affirmation

"I will stand up for justice."

Prayer

Give me courage to stand up for what's right, God.

Amen.

Activity: Role-Play

Role-play a scenario where you need to stand up for a friend.

Day 4: Helping Others Choose Right

Scripture

Galatians 6:2: "Bear ye one another's burdens, and so fulfill the law of Christ" (*Holy Bible NIV: New International Version*, n.d.).

Prayer

Dear Heavenly Father,

Fill me with Your love and compassion, so I can share it generously with those around me. Help me to see the needs of others and to respond with a gentle spirit.

When I encounter someone who is struggling or in pain, empower me to offer support and encouragement.

Let my actions be a light to others, shining Your love in their lives. I trust that with Your help, I can make a positive impact in the lives of those I interact with.

In Jesus' name, I pray,

Amen.

Activity: Challenge

Organize a small group discussion about making right choices.

Day 5: Righteous Actions

Our actions are like signs that show what we believe is right and good! When we choose to do the right thing, like being kind, sharing with others, or helping someone in need, we act righteously. It means we are making choices that reflect love and respect for ourselves and others. Acting righteously helps spread positivity and shows others how to be kind, too. By living this way, we can be examples of goodness and inspire everyone around us to do the same.

Reflection

How can I act righteously?

_____

_____

_____

_____

_____

_____

_____

Scripture

Colossians 3:23: "And whatsoever ye do, do it heartily, as to the Lord, and not unto men" (*Holy Bible NIV: New International Version*, n.d.).

Affirmation

"I will work hard and act righteously!"

Drawing

Draw a large heart with various positive actions depicted inside it, such as helping someone, sharing, praying, and speaking kindly. Surround the heart with rays of light to symbolize how these actions reflect righteousness in God's eyes.

Activity: Challenge

Help with a household task to show righteousness in action.

Day 6: Reflecting on Our Choices

Scripture

Lamentations 3:40: "Let us search and try our ways, and turn again to the Lord" (*Holy Bible NIV: New International Version*, n.d.).

Affirmation

"I will reflect on my choices and improve myself."

Activity: Journaling

Journal about a choice you made and what you learned from it.

Day 7: End-Of-Week Review

- **Recap:** Discuss and share what you've learned from this week's topic with your family.
- **Scripture:** 1 Peter 1:16: "Because it is written, Be ye holy; for I am holy" (*Holy Bible NIV: New International Version*, n.d.).
- **Family Activity:** Create a family bulletin board where everyone can post reminders, affirmations, or goals related to living righteously. Encourage family members to add new items each week, such as Bible verses, quotes, or examples of righteous acts they've seen or accomplished.
- **Preparation for Next Week:** Have you ever done something wrong and felt sorry about it? That feeling is called repentance! It means recognizing when we make a mistake, saying "I'm sorry," and then making a choice to turn away from that wrong behavior. Just like when a car makes a U-turn to go in the right direction, repentance helps us change our course and follow God's way. It's an important part of growing up and becoming better friends, family members, and people. Let's learn more about how we can turn away from wrong and choose to do what's right!

Week 45: Repentance: Turning Away From Wrong

Day 1: Understanding Repentance

Devotion

Repentance means turning away from wrong and asking for forgiveness.

In the Old Testament, a young king named Manasseh ruled over Judah. When he first became king, he did many wrong things that upset God. Instead of following God's commandments, Manasseh turned to idol worship, filled the land with false gods, and even participated in practices that went against everything God had taught His people.

One day, after many years of turning away from God, Manasseh was captured by his enemies and taken to a foreign land as a prisoner. In this dark moment, he realized how far he had strayed from the right path.

In his distress, Manasseh turned to God with a humble heart. He prayed earnestly, confessing his sins and asking for forgiveness. "O Lord, I have sinned against You. Please forgive me!" he cried out. He acknowledged his wrongdoings and pleaded for God's mercy.

God saw Manasseh's sincere heart and heard his prayer. In an amazing act of grace, God restored Manasseh to his kingdom. When he returned to Judah, he made a remarkable change. Manasseh began to undo the wrongs he had done. He removed the idols, repaired the altar of the Lord, and encouraged the people to turn back to worship the one true God.

From that day on, King Manasseh dedicated his life to doing what was right in God's eyes.

Scripture

Acts 3:19: "Repent ye therefore, and be converted, that your sins may be blotted out, when the times of refreshing shall come from the presence of the Lord" (*Holy Bible NIV: New International Version*, n.d.).

Activity: Challenge

Share a time you experienced joy after making things right.

_____

_____

_____

_____

_____

_____

_____

Day 2: God's" Forgiveness

Reflection

Write a list of things you want to change and pray about them.

_____

_____

_____

_____

_____

_____

_____

Scripture

1 John 1:9: "If we confess our sins, he is faithful and just to forgive us our sins, and to cleanse us from all unrighteousness" (*Holy Bible NIV: New International Version*, n.d.).

Affirmation

"I am forgiven because God loves me!"

Activity: Drawing

Draw a heart and write "forgiven" inside it as a reminder of God's love.

Day 3: Making Amends

Discussion

What could you do to make things right with your friends and reconcile with them when there's disagreement?

Scripture

Matthew 5:24: "Leave there thy gift before the altar, and go thy way; first be reconciled to thy brother, and then come and offer thy gift" (*Holy Bible NIV: New International Version*, n.d.).

Activity: Challenge

Think of someone to whom you need to apologize and write them a note.

Day 4: Turning Away From Temptation

Scripture

Matthew 26:41: "Watch and pray, that ye enter not into temptation: the spirit indeed is willing, but the flesh is weak" (*Holy Bible NIV: New International Version*, n.d.).

Prayer

Dear Heavenly Father,

I come to You today seeking Your protection from temptation. I know that there are many challenges and distractions in my life that can lead me away from Your will and purpose. Please help me to be mindful of these temptations and give me the strength to resist them.

Fill my heart with courage and clarity, so I can choose what is right and true. Thank You for Your constant presence and for always being there to support me.

In Jesus' name, I pray,

Amen.

Activity: Challenge

Identify a specific temptation and pray for strength to overcome it.

Day 5: The Joy of Repentance

When we turn back to God, we can find true joy in our hearts! It's like coming home after being away; everything feels warm and right again! God loves us unconditionally and is always ready to welcome us back with open arms. By turning to God, we can experience happiness that lasts, no matter what happens around us!

Reflection

What is true joy when I turn to God?

_____

_____

_____

_____

_____

_____

_____

Scripture

Luke 15:10: "Likewise, I say unto you, there is joy in the presence of the angels of God over one sinner that repenteth" (*Holy Bible NIV: New International Version*, n.d.).

Activity: Drawing

Depict angels in the sky rejoicing and playing musical instruments, surrounded by a beautiful backdrop of clouds and stars. Below them, illustrate a person standing with arms raised, expressing gratitude for forgiveness and joy.

Day 6: Learning From Mistakes

Scripture

Proverbs 24:16: "For a just man falleth seven times, and riseth up again: but the wicked shall fall into mischief" (*Holy Bible NIV: New International Version*, n.d.).

Affirmation

"I learn from my mistakes to grow stronger."

Activity: Journaling

Write in your journal about a past mistake and what you learned from it.

_____

_____

_____

_____

_____

_____

_____

Day 7: Celebrating Forgiveness

- **Recap:** Discuss and share what you've learned from this week's topic with your family.
- **Scripture:** Psalm 103:12: "As far as the east is from the west, so far hath he removed our transgressions from us" (*Holy Bible NIV: New International Version*, n.d.).
- **Family Activity:** Gather with your family members and make a forgiveness board with quotes and scripture about God's forgiveness.
- **Preparation for Next Week:** Have you ever thought about how special your family is? Our families are important because they love us, support us, and help us grow. Just like a team, when we show love and respect in our families, we create a strong bond that helps us work together and overcome challenges.

Week 46: The Importance of Family: Honoring and Respecting Family

Day 1: God's Gift of Family

Devotion

Family is a wonderful gift from God.

Once upon a time in a small village, there lived a kind-hearted woman named Hannah. She had a loving husband, Elkanah, and they were blessed with two sons and a daughter. Their home was filled with laughter, love, and the fragrant aroma of Hannah's cooking.

One day, Hannah felt a deep longing in her heart. She prayed fervently to God for another child, believing that family was a wonderful gift. After many prayers and tears, God honored her request, and Hannah conceived. Overjoyed, she promised to dedicate her child to the Lord.

When Samuel was born, Hannah kept her word. After he was weaned, she took him to the temple and presented him to Eli, the priest, saying, "For this child, I have prayed, and the Lord has granted me my petition." Eli blessed her, and Hannah returned home, knowing she had given her son to fulfill God's purpose.

Years passed, and Samuel grew up to become a great prophet of God, leading the people with wisdom and strength. Hannah visited him each year, bringing gifts and sharing stories of their family. Her heart swelled with pride as she watched Samuel fulfill his calling.

Through Hannah's love and faith, her family knew they were a gift from God—a bond that grew stronger with each passing day.

Scripture

Psalm 127:3: "Children are a heritage from the Lord, offspring a reward from him" (*Holy Bible NIV: New International Version*, n.d.).

Activity: Art and Craft Project

Create a family tree and share it with your family.

Day 2: Honoring Parents

Reflection

We honor our parents by listening and respecting them.

_____

_____

_____

_____

_____

_____

_____

Scripture

Exodus 20:12: "Honor your father and your mother, so that you may live long in the land the Lord your God is giving you" (*Holy Bible NIV: New International Version*, n.d.).

Activity: Challenge

Write a thank-you note to your parents for all they do.

Day 3: Helping Family Members

Discussion

How can we help our family by showing kindness?

Scripture

Galatians 5:13: "You, my brothers and sisters, were called to be free. But do not use your freedom to indulge the flesh; rather, serve one another humbly in love" (*Holy Bible NIV: New International Version*, n.d.).

Activity: Challenge

Pick a chore to do for a family member today.

Day 4: Family Time

Scripture

Ecclesiastes 4:9-10: "Two are better than one, because they have a good return for their labor: If either of them falls down, one can help the other up. But pity anyone who falls and has no one to help them" (*Holy Bible NIV: New International Version*, n.d.).

Prayer

Dear God,

Thank You for our family and the special times we share together. Help us to fill our hearts with love, kindness, and laughter.

May we always support and encourage each other, and cherish every memory we create. Guide us to be patient and understanding, and remind us to say "I love you" often.

Thank You for the gift of family. We love You, God!

In Your Holy Name,

Amen.

Activity: Challenge

Plan a fun family activity for the week.

Day 5: Listening to Each Other

Listening is a super important way to show respect to our family! When we listen, we pay attention to what our parents, siblings, or relatives are saying, just like we want them to listen to us. It shows that we care about their thoughts and feelings, and it helps us understand each other better. Being a good listener shows that we love and respect our family members.

Reflection

How can I become a better listener to my surroundings?

_____

_____

_____

_____

_____

_____

_____

Scripture

James 1:19: "My dear brothers and sisters, take note of this: Everyone should be quick to listen, slow to speak, and slow to become angry" (*Holy Bible NIV: New International Version*, n.d.).

Activity: Drawing

Draw a big garden with different colorful flowers representing each family member or friend. Each flower can have a face and a speech bubble. In the speech bubble, they can write something they like or appreciate about listening (e.g., "I feel heard!" or "Listening helps us understand each other!"). Add garden features like butterflies and bees that represent positive communication, flying around the flowers, showing that listening helps ideas flourish.

Day 6: Family Traditions

Scripture

Deuteronomy 6:7: "Impress them on your children. Talk about them when you sit at home and when you walk along the road, when you lie down and when you get up" (*Holy Bible NIV: New International Version*, n.d.).

Affirmation

"I cherish our family traditions."

Activity: Challenge

Write down your favorite family traditions and share them.

_____
_____
_____
_____
_____
_____
_____

Day 7: End-Of-Week Review

- **Recap:** Discuss and share what you've learned from this week's topic with your family.
- **Scripture:** 1 Thessalonians 5:17: "Pray continually" (*Holy Bible NIV: New International Version*, n.d.).
- **Family Activity:** Create a family prayer list and pray for each member by name.
- **Preparation for Next Week:** Just like a compass helps us find our way, God wants to help us make good choices and lead us on the right path. When we turn to Him in prayer, read the Bible, and listen to our hearts, we can discover what He wants for us. By seeking His guidance, we can navigate through challenges, make wise decisions, and grow closer to Him every day!

Week 47: Guidance: Seeking God's Direction

Day 1: Listening to God

Devotion

God wants us to listen to Him so He can guide our paths.

Once upon a time, in a quaint village, there lived a young boy named John. John was known for his quick wit and adventurous spirit. However, he often rushed into decisions without seeking advice, which sometimes led him to trouble.

One day, John decided to venture deep into the forest, attracted by the sounds of a beautiful stream. His mother warned him, "Make sure to follow the path and listen to God's voice; He will guide you safely." But John, excited and curious, hurried along, ignoring her words.

As he wandered, he soon found himself lost. The trees looked unfamiliar, and the sun began to set, casting shadows all around him. Panic set in, and John realized he hadn't stopped to listen to his heart or seek God's guidance.

Feeling scared and alone, he knelt down and prayed, asking God for help. Quietly, as he listened, he felt a gentle nudge in his heart. Remembering the way he came, he turned back—this time, with patience, paying attention to the signs around him.

After some time, John finally saw the familiar path leading toward home. Relieved, he ran back, grateful that he had taken a moment to listen. From that day on, John understood the importance of seeking God's guidance and listening for His voice, knowing it would lead him safely through life's adventures.

Scripture

Proverbs 3:5-6: "Trust in the Lord with all your heart and lean not on your own understanding; in all your ways submit to him, and he will make your paths straight" (*Holy Bible NIV: New International Version*, n.d.).

Activity: Meditation

Spend quiet time outdoors and listen for God's guidance.

Day 2: Praying for Direction

Scripture

Psalm 32:8: "I will instruct you and teach you in the way you should go; I will counsel you with my loving eye on you" (*Holy Bible NIV: New International Version*, n.d.).

Affirmation

"God teaches me the best way to live."

Activity: Prayer

Write a short prayer asking God for guidance in a specific situation.

_____

_____

_____

_____

_____

_____

_____

Day 3: Trusting in God's Plan

Discussion

How can I trust God even if I don't understand his Plans for me?

Scripture

Jeremiah 29:11: "For I know the plans I have for you, declares the Lord, plans to prosper you and not to harm you, plans to give you hope and a future" (*Holy Bible NIV: New International Version*, n.d.).

Activity: Art and Craft Project

Create a vision board that reflects what you hope for, trusting God's plans.

Day 4: Reading Scripture for Wisdom

Scripture

2 Timothy 3:16-17: "All Scripture is God-breathed and is useful for teaching, rebuking, correcting and training in righteousness, so that the servant of God may be thoroughly equipped for every good work" (*Holy Bible NIV: New International Version*, n.d.).

Prayer

Dear Lord,

Thank You for the gift of Your Word, which teaches and guides us every day. May Your scriptures inspire me to grow in wisdom, kindness, and love. Help me to remember the lessons I learn, applying them to my life and sharing them with others.

Thank You for being my teacher and for leading me on the right path. I trust in Your guidance and embrace the journey of learning from You.

In Jesus' Name,

Amen.

Activity: Challenge

Pick a Bible story and discuss how it provides guidance.

Day 5: Following God's Path

God's way is the best path for us to follow because He knows what's best for our lives! Just like a wise guide leading us on an adventure, God gives us rules and teachings to help us make good choices. God's way teaches us to be kind, honest, and caring toward others. Sometimes, we might want to do things our own way, but God's way leads us to joy and keeps us safe.

Reflection

God's way is the best way for us to follow.

_____

_____

_____

_____

_____

_____

_____

Scripture

Psalm 119:105: "Your word is a lamp for my feet, a light on my path" (*Holy Bible NIV: New International Version*, n.d.).

Activity: Drawing

Draw your own path and mark how you'll follow God's direction this week.

Day 6: Seeking Help From Others

Scripture

Proverbs 15:22: "Plans fail for lack of counsel, but with many advisers, they succeed" (*Holy Bible NIV: New International Version*, n.d.).

Affirmation

"I learn from my family and friends."

Activity: Challenge

Talk to a family member about a decision you need help with.

Day 7: End-Of-Week Review

- **Recap:** Discuss and share what you've learned from this week's topic with your family.
- **Scripture:** Psalm 46:10: "Be still, and know that I am God; I will be exalted among the nations, I will be exalted in the earth" (*Holy Bible NIV: New International Version*, n.d.).

- **Activity:** As a family, discuss moments when you felt God's guidance in your lives. Think about decisions you made, challenges you faced, or times you found comfort in prayer.
- **Preparation for Next Week:** Just like different colors come together to make a beautiful rainbow, people can join forces to create something wonderful. When we listen to one another, share our ideas, and support each other, we can achieve great things and make our world a better place.

Week 48: Unity: Working Together in Love

Day 1: The Power of Togetherness

Devotion

God wants us to work together in love and support one another.

Once upon a time, in a small village, there lived a group of children who loved to play together but often argued over who would lead their games. One sunny afternoon, they gathered in a beautiful meadow to decide what to play. Julia wanted to play tag, while Jacob preferred hide-and-seek. The arguing went on until an elder named Elijah approached them.

With a warm smile, Elijah shared a story from the Bible about how God created the world and everything in it, reminding them that each part plays a special role. He said, "Just like different colors make a beautiful painting, each of you brings something unique to our games. When you work together, you can create something even more fun!"

Inspired by Elijah's words, the children decided to combine their ideas. They created a new game that included elements from both tag and hide and seek, where one child would tag others but also give them secret hiding spots in the meadow. They laughed and cheered as they played, realizing how much better it was to support each other and work together.

From that day on, the children's friendship grew stronger, and they remembered Elijah's message. They learned that working together in love made their games more joyful and their bond unbreakable.

Scripture

Ephesians 4:3: "Make every effort to keep the unity of the Spirit through the bond of peace" (*Holy Bible NIV: New International Version*, n.d.).

Activity: Challenge

Discuss with your family or friends what unity means to you.

Day 2: Helping One Another

Reflection

How can I use my gifts to help my family every day?

_____

_____

_____

_____

_____

_____

_____

Scripture

1 Corinthians 12:12: "Just as a body, though one, has many parts, but all its many parts form one body, so it is with Christ" (*Holy Bible NIV: New International Version*, n.d.).

Activity: Challenge

Find a small service project to do with your family or friends.

Day 3: Speaking Kind Words

Discussion

What are the best ways to speak with kindness, and what words should we use more often to nurture our relationships with others?

Scripture

Proverbs 16:24: "Gracious words are a honeycomb, sweet to the soul and healing to the bones" (*Holy Bible NIV: New International Version*, n.d.).

Activity: Challenge

Create a "kindness jar" where everyone writes a kind word or phrase to share.

Day 4: Working on a Team

Scripture

Philippians 1:27: "Whatever happens, conduct yourselves in a manner worthy of the gospel of Christ. Then, whether I come and see you or only hear about you in my absence, I will know that you stand firm in the one Spirit, striving together as one for the faith of the gospel" (*Holy Bible NIV: New International Version*, n.d.).

Prayer

Dear God,

Help me to be a good team player, filled with kindness and love. Teach me to listen to others and value their ideas, and encourage them in their endeavors.

Let my words be uplifting and my actions reflect Your love, so that we may grow in harmony and togetherness.

In Your Holy Name,

Amen.

Activity: Challenge

Play a team game or sport with friends, focusing on working together.

Day 5: Accepting Differences

Everyone is unique, which means we all have different qualities that make us special, like how some of us are great at sports while others love to draw or sing. Embracing our differences means celebrating what makes us unique instead of focusing on what divides us. When we come together in unity, we can learn from each other and build strong friendships.

Journaling

Everyone is unique, and we can embrace our differences in unity. Write down a list of qualities that make you different.

_____

_____

_____

_____

_____

_____

_____

Scripture

Colossians 3:14: "And over all these virtues put on love, which binds them all together in perfect unity" (*Holy Bible NIV: New International Version*, n.d.).

Activity: Art and Craft Project

Create a craft that represents the uniqueness of your friends or family members.

Day 6: Praying for Unity

Scripture

John 17:21: "That all of them may be one, Father, just as you are in me and I am in you. May they also be in us so that the world may believe that you have sent me" (*Holy Bible NIV: New International Version*, n.d.).

Affirmation

"I pray for unity among my friends and family!"

Activity: Prayer

Have a family prayer time, asking God for unity and love in your community.

Day 7: End-Of-Week Review

- **Recap:** Discuss and share what you've learned from this week's topic with your family.
- **Scripture:** Romans 15:5-6: "May the God who gives endurance and encouragement give you the same attitude of mind toward each other that Christ Jesus had, so that with one mind and

one voice you may glorify the God and Father of our Lord Jesus Christ" (*Holy Bible NIV: New International Version*, n.d.).

- **Family Activity:** As a family or group, discuss what you've learned about unity this week.
- **Preparation for Next Week:** Redemption is all about the incredible power of a second chance! Imagine making a mistake, like forgetting to do your homework or accidentally hurting a friend's feelings. Redemption teaches us that mistakes are a part of growing up, and what truly matters is how we learn from them and make them right.

Week 49: Redemption: The Power of a Second Chance

Day 1: Understanding Redemption

Devotion

Redemption means God gives us a second chance, no matter what we've done.

In a vibrant village, there lived a man named Jonah who was known for his sharp temper. He often shouted at neighbors and was quick to judge others, leading to a life filled with loneliness. One day, while wandering through the marketplace, Jonah heard a group of children excitedly recounting the story of Zacchaeus, a man who made mistakes and was disliked by many. Yet, when Jesus saw him, He offered Zacchaeus friendship and a chance to change.

Later that evening, he knelt by his bed and prayed, asking God for forgiveness and the strength to be a better person. The next day, Jonah decided to reach out to those he had wronged. He started with Mrs. Patel, an elderly neighbor at whom he had often snapped. Approaching her door, he hesitated, fearing rejection, but then knocked gently and apologized.

To his surprise, Mrs. Patel welcomed him with open arms, saying, "It takes courage to ask for forgiveness. We all deserve a second chance." Encouraged by her kindness, Jonah continued to mend his relationships. With each apology, he felt a weight lifted from his heart.

As time passed, Jonah transformed from a man filled with bitterness to one overflowing with love and compassion. He realized that redemption was not just a gift he received from God but a path he could walk to share that love with others.

Scripture

Ephesians 1:7: "In Him, we have redemption through His blood, the forgiveness of sins, in accordance with the riches of God's grace" (*Holy Bible NIV: New International Version*, n.d.).

Activity: Journaling

Journal about a time when you received or extended forgiveness.

_____
_____
_____
_____
_____
_____
_____

Day 2: Learning From Mistakes

Scripture

Proverbs 24:16: "For though the righteous fall seven times, they rise again, but the wicked stumble when calamity strikes" (*Holy Bible NIV: New International Version*, n.d.).

Affirmation

"I can learn and grow from my mistakes."

Activity: Reflection

Write down something you learned from a mistake you made.

_____
_____
_____

_____

_____

_____

_____

Day 3: Forgiving Others

Discussion

What does forgiveness mean, and how can we apply it to our interactions with our friends and families?

Scripture

Colossians 3:13: "Bear with each other and forgive one another if any of you has a grievance against someone. Forgive as the Lord forgave you" (*Holy Bible NIV: New International Version*, n.d.).

Activity: Art and Craft Project

Create a "Forgiving Hearts" craft, representing the forgiveness you give to others.

Day 4: Accepting God's" Forgiveness

Scripture

Romans 5:8: "But God demonstrates His own love for us in this: While we were still sinners, Christ died for us" (*Holy Bible NIV: New International Version*, n.d.).

Prayer

Dear Heavenly Father,

Thank You for loving me, even when I fall short and stumble along the way. Your unwavering love lifts me in my darkest moments and fills my heart with hope.

I am grateful for Your grace that embraces my imperfections and reminds me that I am cherished just as I am.

Help me to learn from my mistakes and grow stronger in faith, knowing that Your love never wavers.

In Jesus' Name,

Amen.

Activity: Art and Craft Project

Create a card that reflects your journey of redemption and decorate it!

Day 5: Sharing the Message of Redemption

Redemption is like getting a second chance after making a mistake. We can explain to our friends that no matter what they've done, God loves them and wants to help them become better. We can share stories about how Jesus showed love and forgiveness, reminding them that they can always turn to God for help and guidance. By sharing this message, we can inspire our friends to feel hope and understand how special they are to God!

Reflection

Reflect and write in your journal about how it feels to be forgiven by God.

_____

_____

_____

_____

Scripture

Mark 16:15: "He said to them, 'Go into all the world and preach the gospel to all creation'" (*Holy Bible NIV: New International Version*, n.d.).

Activity: Drawing

Draw a picture to share the message of redemption with someone.

Day 6: The Joy of a Second Chance

Scripture

Luke 15:10: "In the same way, I tell you, there is rejoicing in the presence of the angels of God over one sinner who repents" (*Holy Bible NIV: New International Version*, n.d.).

Affirmation

"I celebrate new beginnings!"

Activity: Challenge

Plan a small celebration at home or with friends for new beginnings.

Day 7: Reflecting on Redemption

- **Recap:** Discuss and share what you've learned from this week's topic with your family.
- **Scripture:** 2 Corinthians 5:17: "Therefore, if anyone is in Christ, the new creation has come: The old has gone, the new is here" (*Holy Bible NIV: New International Version*, n.d.).
- **Family Activity:** Pass around a soft object, such as a small pillow or stuffed animal. When someone holds the object, it's their turn to share a time they've experienced forgiveness or a moment when they needed a second chance.
- **Preparation for Next Week:** The Fruit of the Spirit refers to the special qualities that help us live in a way that makes God proud! When we let God's spirit work in our hearts, we can show love, joy, peace, patience, kindness, goodness, faithfulness, gentleness, and self-control. These qualities help us to be better friends, support one another, and make our world a brighter place.

Week 50: The Fruit of the Spirit: Living With Godly Qualities

Day 1: What Is the Fruit of the Spirit?

Devotion

The Fruit of the Spirit are qualities God wants us to show.

In the peaceful village of Hopevale, the air was always filled with laughter, and the gardens bloomed with vibrant colors. The villagers believed that their harmony came from the values they cherished, particularly the virtues known as the "Fruit of the Spirit." These qualities—love, joy, peace, patience, kindness, goodness, faithfulness, gentleness, and self-control—were at the very core of their community.

One day, a traveling merchant named Abel visited Hopevale. Curious to learn more, he began talking to the villagers about their secret to such happiness.

An elder named Esther, who had lived in Hopevale for many years, invited Abel to stay for the village's annual Harvest Festival.

As the day approached, the villagers began preparing. Esther coordinated the events, ensuring that everyone contributed. She embodied love as she encouraged the shy children to share their talents.

On the day of the festival, joy echoed throughout the village as laughter filled the air. Children danced and played games while the aroma of delicious food wafted from every home. Abel watched as kindness unfolded all around him—neighbors sharing their harvests and helping each other with preparations.

In one corner, a young boy named Jacob exhibited extraordinary patience while helping his mother decorate the main hall. Despite the chaos of the preparations, he remained calm and cheerful, inspiring those around him.

As the festivities continued, Abel noticed a girl named Lily sitting alone, her face reflecting sadness. Moved by her loneliness, he approached her with a gentle smile. "What's the matter?" he asked. Lily shared that she felt out of place and had trouble making friends. Abel, showing gentleness, encouraged her to take a deep breath and offered to introduce her to other children.

With his help, Lily joined in the games and soon found herself surrounded by laughter and new friends. Clara, a kind-hearted girl, welcomed her with open arms, demonstrating the very essence of kindness.

As the sun set, the village gathered for a communal feast. Abel was amazed at how faithfulness shone through the villagers' camaraderie—they stood by each other in both good times and bad. As they shared stories of their challenges and victories, Abel realized that the bonds among them were rooted in their commitment to uphold these virtues.

After the feast, the villagers shared what the Fruit of the Spirit meant to them. One by one, they spoke of how these qualities shaped their community and their lives. The conversation sparked a lively debate, where villagers enthusiastically exchanged ideas about how to nurture these virtues further.

By the end of the night, Abel felt a profound sense of belonging. Before departing, he stood before the villagers and expressed, "You have taught me that the true wealth of a community lies not in its possessions but in the love and kindness it shows one another. In my travels, I often sought riches, but now I see that the Fruit of the Spirit is the most precious gift of all."

Scripture

Galatians 5:22-23: "But the fruit of the Spirit is love, joy, peace, forbearance, kindness, goodness, faithfulness, gentleness, and self-control. Against such things, there is no law" (*Holy Bible NIV: New International Version*, n.d.).

Activity: Art and Craft Project

Create a colorful poster displaying the nine fruits of the Spirit.

Day 2: The Importance of Love

Scripture

1 Corinthians 13:4-5: "Love is patient, love is kind. It does not envy, it does not boast, it is not proud. It does not dishonor others, it is not self-seeking, it is not easily angered, it keeps no record of wrongs" (*Holy Bible NIV: New International Version*, n.d.).

Affirmation

"I choose to love like Jesus!"

Activity: Reflection

Write down ways you can show love to your family and friends.

_____

_____

_____

_____

_____

_____

_____

Day 3: Experiencing Joy

Discussion

How can we choose to find joy in serving God?

Scripture

Nehemiah 8:10: "Nehemiah said, 'Go and enjoy choice food and sweet drinks, and send some to those who have nothing prepared. This day is sacred to our Lord. Do not grieve, for the joy of the Lord is your strength'" (*Holy Bible NIV: New International Version*, n.d.).

Activity: Journaling

Create a "Joy Journal" where you write about things that make you happy.

Day 4: Practicing Peace

Scripture

Philippians 4:7: "And the peace of God, which transcends all understanding, will guard your hearts and your minds in Christ Jesus" (*Holy Bible NIV: New International Version*, n.d.).

Prayer

Dear Heavenly Father,

Help me to let go of the burdens I carry and trust in Your perfect plan for my life.

As I breathe deeply, let Your peace wash over me like a gentle stream, calming my spirit and soothing my mind. Remind me that in moments of turmoil, I can find solace in You.

I ask for Your guidance in all areas of my life.

Thank You for Your endless love and grace. I trust in Your promise to give me rest and restoration.

Amen.

Activity: Meditation

Practice a short meditation time, focusing on God's presence.

Day 5: Kindness Matters

Kindness is a powerful way to make a big difference in someone's day! When we do something nice for others, like sharing our toys, helping a friend, or giving a compliment, it can make them feel happy and cared for. For example, if we smile at someone or ask how they are doing, it can brighten their mood right away! Kindness is like a little spark that can spread joy to everyone around us.

Reflection

Kindness can change someone's day. What can I do each day to show kindness?

_____
_____
_____
_____
_____
_____
_____
_____

Scripture

Ephesians 4:32: "Be kind and compassionate to one another, forgiving each other, just as in Christ God forgave you" (*Holy Bible NIV: New International Version*, n.d.).

Activity: Drawing

Draw various community helpers, like firefighters, teachers, and nurses, showing how their kindness impacts the community.

Day 6: Being Gentle

Scripture

Philippians 4:5: "Let your gentleness be evident to all. The Lord is near." (*Holy Bible NIV: New International Version.*, n.d.)

Affirmation

"I am gentle with my words and actions."

Activity: Reflection

Reflect on a time you were able to be gentle and how it helped someone.

_____
_____
_____
_____
_____
_____
_____

Day 7: Celebrating the Fruit of the Spirit

- **Recap:** Discuss and share what you've learned from this week's topic with your family.

- **Scripture:** John 15:8: "This is to my Father's glory, that you bear much fruit, showing yourselves to be my disciples" (*Holy Bible NIV: New International Version*, n.d.).
- **Family Activity:** Create a fruit-themed craft that represents the Fruit of the Spirit.
- **Preparation for Next Week:** The Good Shepherd is a special name for Jesus that shows how much He loves and cares for us! Just like a shepherd takes care of their sheep, guiding and protecting them, Jesus watches over each one of us with kindness and compassion. He knows when we're happy, sad, or even lost, and He is always there to help us find our way. Jesus teaches us about love, friendship, and being there for others, reminding us that we are never alone. With Jesus as our Good Shepherd, we can trust that we are safe and cherished every day!

Week 51: The Good Shepherd: Jesus' Care for Us

Day 1: Who Is the Good Shepherd?

Devotion

Jesus is like a shepherd who cares deeply for us.

A kindhearted shepherd named Thomas lived in the quaint village of Oakridge, nestled between lush green hills and blooming wildflowers.

One sunny morning, as golden rays bathed the hills, Thomas led his flock to a new meadow he had discovered—the grass was fresh and plentiful, perfect for grazing. As the sheep scattered across the field, content and happy, Thomas carefully watched over them, enjoying the peace of the moment.

But as he surveyed the meadow, Thomas noticed a little lamb named Grace, who seemed hesitant to join the others. She looked around nervously, her eyes wide with confusion. Thomas walked over, kneeling beside her. "What's wrong, little one?" he asked gently.

"I don't know if I can find my way back if I leave this spot," Grace replied, her tiny voice trembling. "What if I get lost?"

Thomas smiled warmly, placing a reassuring hand on her back. "You are never alone, Grace. I am your shepherd, and I will always lead you back to safety. Trust in me." With that, he took her small hoof in his hand and guided her toward the rest of the flock.

As the rain began to pour, one little lamb—a curious one named Leo—wandered away, frightened by the noise of the thunder. Thomas's heart sank as he realized Leo was missing. "Stay here, all of you!" he instructed the remaining sheep, and without a moment's hesitation, he dashed into the storm, calling for Leo.

"Leo! Where are you?" he shouted, his voice nearly drowned out by the roaring winds.

"Leo!" he exclaimed, and there, trembling beneath a bush, was the little lamb. Thomas rushed to his side. "I found you! You don't need to be afraid. I'm here!" He scooped Leo into his arms, holding him close, and together, they returned to the safety of the flock.

Once the storm passed and the sun reappeared, casting a rainbow across the sky, Thomas looked at his sheep, knowing the bond they shared was unbreakable. They were never truly lost when they followed their shepherd.

Scripture

John 10:11: "I am the good shepherd. The good shepherd lays down his life for the sheep" (Holy Bible NIV: New International Version, n.d.).

Activity: Drawing

Draw or color a picture of a shepherd with sheep.

Day 2: Trusting Jesus' Guidance

Reflection

How can I trust Jesus to guide me like a shepherd?

_____

_____

_____

_____

_____

_____

Scripture

Psalm 23:1: "The Lord is my shepherd, I lack nothing" (*Holy Bible NIV: New International Version*, n.d.).

Activity: Drawing

Create a path on paper, drawing where you want to follow Jesus this week.

Day 3: Jesus Protects Us

Discussion

The Good Shepherd protects His sheep from harm. What does it mean to have Jesus' protection for all your life?

Scripture

Psalm 23:4: "Even though I walk through the darkest valley, I will fear no evil, for you are with me; your rod and your staff, they comfort me" (*Holy Bible NIV: New International Version*, n.d.).

Activity: Reflection

Write down the ways Jesus has protected you in your life.

_____

_____

_____

_____

_____

_____

Day 4: Finding Comfort in Jesus

Scripture

Matthew 28:20: "And surely I am with you always, to the very end of the age" (*Holy Bible NIV: New International Version*, n.d.).

Prayer

Dear Lord,

Thank You for Your constant presence in my life. I am grateful that You are always with me, guiding me through every challenge and joy I face.

Help me to feel Your comforting presence in my heart, reassuring me that I am never alone. Thank You for being my constant companion.

In Your Holy Name,

Amen.

Activity: Meditation

Spend time meditating quietly, feeling His presence and comfort.

Day 5: Caring for Others

Just like Jesus, we are called to care for the people around us! Jesus showed love and kindness to everyone, helping those who were sick, lonely, or in need. When we care for others, we show that we love them too. This can be done by being a good friend, helping our family, or even just listening when someone needs to talk.

Journaling

Like Jesus, we are here to care for those around us. List actions that show how meaningful our surroundings are to us.

_____

_____

_____

_____

_____

_____

Scripture

John 15:13: "Greater love has no one than this: to lay down one's life for one's friends" (*Holy Bible NIV: New International Version*, n.d.).

Affirmation

"I care for others just like Jesus cares for me!"

Activity: Drawing

Create a drawing of a small gift or treat for someone you care about.

Day 6: Following the Shepherd's Voice

Scripture

John 10:27: "My sheep hear my voice, and I know them, and they follow me" (*Holy Bible NIV: New International Version*, n.d.).

Affirmation

"I hear and follow Jesus' voice!"

Activity: Prayer

Spend time in prayer, asking for clarity in what you hear from Jesus.

Day 7: End-Of-Week Review

- **Recap:** Discuss and share what you've learned from this week's topic with your family.
- **Scripture:** 1 John 3:16: "This is how we know what love is: Jesus Christ laid down his life for us. And we ought to lay down our lives for our brothers and sisters." (*Holy Bible NIV: New International Version.*, n.d.)
- **Family Activity:** Create a thank-you card for Jesus, expressing your gratitude.
- **Preparation for Next Week:** The commission is an exciting topic that teaches us about sharing God's message with everyone around the world! Think of it as a special mission from God, inviting us to be His messengers. Just like superheroes spread hope and love, we can tell others about God's amazing love and how He wants everyone to be friends with Him. Whether it's through kind words, helping hands, or sharing stories of faith, we each have a part to play in this wonderful mission. God believes in us, and He is counting on us to spread joy and love far and wide, uniting people in His care!

Week 52: Commission: Sharing God's Message Worldwide

Day 1: What Is the Great Commission?

Devotion

Jesus calls us to share His message of love with the world.

In a quiet village surrounded by gentle hills, there lived a kind-hearted woman named Mary. Every morning, she would walk to the well to draw water, often stopping to greet her neighbors with a warm smile or a kind word. Yet, she noticed a man named Simon, who lived on the outskirts, rarely left his home and seemed troubled.

One day, inspired by the teachings of Jesus, Mary decided to reach out to Simon. She baked a batch of her famous bread and walked to his house, her heart pounding with both excitement and apprehension. As she approached, she found Simon sitting on his doorstep, staring off into the distance.

"Good morning, Simon!" Mary called out cheerfully. He looked up, surprised but intrigued by her presence. "I brought you some bread. Would you like to share a meal with me?"

Simon hesitated but then nodded, grateful for the gesture. As they shared the bread, Mary spoke of the beauty of community, of how Jesus taught us to love and support one another. She listened as Simon opened up about his struggles and the loneliness he had faced since losing his wife.

With each story shared, a bond began to form. Mary encouraged Simon to participate in village gatherings, reminding him that he was valued and loved. Inspired by Mary's kindness, Simon slowly began to venture out, joining in the village life.

Over time, he found purpose in helping others, sharing his experiences and the love he had received from Mary.

Scripture

Matthew 28:19-20: "Therefore go and make disciples of all nations, baptizing them in the name of the Father and of the Son and of the Holy Spirit, and teaching them to obey everything I have commanded you. And surely I am with you always, to the very end of the age" (*Holy Bible NIV: New International Version*, n.d.).

Activity: Art and Craft Project

Create a world map and mark places you want to share God's" love.

Day 2: Telling Friends About Jesus

Scripture

Acts 1:8: "But you will receive power when the Holy Spirit comes on you; and you will be my witnesses in Jerusalem, and in all Judea and Samaria, and to the ends of the earth" (*Holy Bible NIV: New International Version*, n.d.).

Affirmation

"I will tell my friends about Jesus!"

Activity: Journaling

Write a letter sharing what Jesus means to you.

_____

_____

_____

_____

_____

_____

Day 3: Serving Others in Love

Discussion

Discuss why serving others shows God's love and opens doors to share the Gospel.

Scripture

Galatians 5:13: "You, my brothers and sisters, were called to be free. But do not use your freedom to indulge the flesh; rather, serve one another humbly in love" (*Holy Bible NIV: New International Version*, n.d.).

Activity: Challenge

Plan a small service project to help someone in need.

Day 4: Praying for the World

Scripture

1 Timothy 2:1: "I urge, then, first of all, that petitions, prayers, intercession, and thanksgiving be made for all people" (*Holy Bible NIV: New International Version*, n.d.).

Prayer

Dear God,

We know that Your message of love is important, and we want to share it with others. Please help us to remember those who need to hear about You.

Help us to be brave and kind, so we can tell our friends and family about Your love.

We pray for everyone who doesn't know You yet. Help them feel Your love and comfort.

Thank You, God, for being with us as we share Your message.

In Jesus' Name,

Amen.

Activity: Prayer

Create a prayer list for people and places where God's message needs to be shared.

Day 5: Living Out the Great Commission

We can live our lives in a way that shows Jesus' love every day by being kind and caring to everyone we meet! This means being helpful to our friends, forgiving others when they make mistakes, and sharing our toys or treats with those in need. Remember, every day is an opportunity to show others how much they matter, and by doing so, we share the love of Jesus with the world!

Reflection

How can I live my life in a way that reflects Jesus' love every day?

_____

_____

_____

_____

_____

_____

_____

Scripture

Matthew 5:16: "In the same way, let your light shine before others, that they may see your good deeds and glorify your Father in heaven" (*Holy Bible NIV: New International Version*, n.d.).

Activity: Drawing

Create a drawing showing kindness in your daily interactions.

Day 6: Sharing Faith Stories

Scripture

Psalm 107:2: "Let the redeemed of the Lord tell their story—those he redeemed from the hand of the foe" (*Holy Bible NIV: New International Version*, n.d.).

Affirmation

"My story can lead others to Jesus!"

Activity: Challenge

Write down your faith story and practice sharing it with a family member.

_____

_____

_____

_____

_____

_____

_____

Day 7: End-Of-Week Review

- **Recap:** Discuss and share what you've learned from this week's topic with your family.
- **Scripture:** Luke 10:2: "He told them, 'The harvest is plentiful, but the workers are few. Ask the Lord of the harvest, therefore, to send out workers into his harvest field'" (*Holy Bible NIV: New International Version*, n.d.).
- **Family Activity:** Create a fun celebration (like a small party) to encourage others to share the love of Jesus, too!

Conclusion

Congratulations on making it to the end of this incredible journey! Over the past 52 weeks, you've explored so many valuable lessons that can shape who you are and how you interact with the world around you.

Now, take a moment to remember some of your favorite lessons. For instance, learning to seek God's direction isn't just about knowing the right choices to make now but also about trusting that you'll be guided throughout your entire life.

What if we think about these lessons as seeds planted in a garden? When you plant a seed, you water it, give it sunlight, and watch it grow. The same goes for these values. If you continue to practice faithfulness, kindness, patience, and all the other virtues, they will blossom within you. Whatever season of life you're in, whether it's starting a new school year, making new friends, or even when you face challenges, these principles will guide you.

Remember our lesson on living with godly qualities? What if everyone in your family took turns sharing ways they've practiced those qualities during the week? It could ignite a wonderful spark of service, love, and understanding in your household.

To make sure these lessons stay with you, consider keeping a journal. Writing down your thoughts, feelings, and the progress you make can be incredibly helpful.

As you step forward, remember that every small act of kindness, every decision to tell the truth, and every effort to be patient shapes the amazing person you are becoming. Life is full of opportunities to practice what you've learned. Whether it's standing up for someone, listening when someone needs to talk, or simply being there for a friend, these actions make a big difference.

Even though this book may come to an end, your journey continues. Keep revisiting the lessons, maybe once a month or whenever you feel the need for a little guidance. You can always look back at your notes, discuss these values with people you trust, and find new ways to apply them as you grow older.

So here's to you for all the hard work, dedication, and heart you've put into this journey. You're equipped with tools that will serve you well throughout your entire life. Keep learning, keep growing, and keep spreading kindness wherever you go. The world is a better place with you in it, living out these cherished values. Happy adventures ahead, dear reader, and never stop celebrating the amazing person you are!

References

Holy Bible NIV: New international version. (n.d.). Christian Media Bibles.

Milton Keynes UK
Ingram Content Group UK Ltd.
UKHW051536301124
451951UK00006B/53

9 798991 792653